The Hundred Year Stretch and Beyond

Doris Chapin Bailey

Order this book online at www.trafford.com
or email orders@trafford.com

Most Trafford titles are also available at major online book retailers.

Print information available on the last page.

ISBN: 978-1-4907-7263-9 (sc)
ISBN: 978-1-4907-7262-2 (e)

Trafford rev.   05/11/2016

Trafford
PUBLISHING®   www.trafford.com
North America & international
toll-free: 1 888 232 4444 (USA & Canada)
fax: 812 355 4082

AUTHOR'S NOTE:

The following autobiography by J.H. Andersen has been included by the author in this book because she found it in her grandparents' memorabilia while working on this book, he has always been a person whom she had admired and loved and this was a way to show her love and respect for this man, and his importance to her life, as well as his amazing wit.

Doris Marie Chapin Nanney Bailey

THIS BOOK IS DEDICATED WITH LOVE TO:

MY FOUR CHILDREN:

GAYLEEN RENÉ JACOBS
ANITA HOWARD LEONARD
JANICE DIANE WALKER
JOHN ELLIS NANNEY

Who gave me unconditional encouragement and love while it was being written. Their care and understanding has meant more to me than can be said. Their love, care and acceptance of Roy has been the best gift they could have ever given me. I have been blessed.

Thank you.

Doris Marie Chapin Nanney Bailey

ACKNOWLEDGEMENTS

What a lot of wonderful encouragement I received while writing this story of my life and those who were my forebears. Amazing people were these people who came ahead of me. What I have learned about them and their lives has been fascinating. I am lucky to have inherited their genes. There are two people without whom I could not have finished this book. I worked in the office at the local high school for several years. My friend was an English teacher there. She volunteered to proof my manuscript for me and although she did not have time to do a complete editing, she did some of that too. Dorothy Orbison has a kind and giving heart and she gave me her expertise and many kind words. I am greatly thankful for her thoughtful critique and especially for correcting all my punctuation. She gave me the ability to make a better work.

And, the second person was my daughter, Jan, who did all the magical electronic work. She worked tirelessly and without her this book would not have all the many things that make a book not only beautiful but professional. She did all the picture enhancement and conversion, combined pages, created tables including a table of contents and arranged the genealogy so that it was readable and could be followed. My profound thanks go to these women who gave me so much time and love. If this book gives a pleasing feel it is because of their care. Thank you.

Doris Chapin Bailey

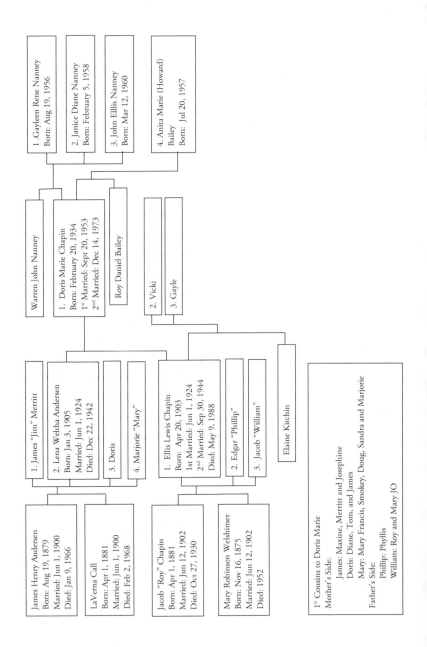

1. Gayleen Rene Nanney
Born: Aug 19, 1956

2. Janice Diane Nanney
Born: February 5, 1958

3. John Elllis Nanney
Born: Mar 12, 1960

4. Anita Marie (Howard) Bailey
Born: Jul 20, 1957

Warren John Nanney

1. Doris Marie Chapin
Born: February 20, 1934
1st Married: Sept 20, 1953
2nd Married: Dec 14, 1973

Roy Daniel Bailey

2. Vicki

3. Gayle

1. James "Jim" Merritt

2. Lena Weltha Andersen
Born: Jan 3, 1905
Married: Jun 1, 1924
Died: Dec 22, 1942

3. Doris

4. Marjorie "Mary"

1. Ellis Lewis Chapin
Born: Apr 20, 1903
1st Married: Jun 1, 1924
2nd Married: Sep 30, 1944
Died: May 9, 1988

2. Edgar "Phillip"

3. Jacob "William"

Elaine Kitchin

James Henry Andersen
Born: Aug 19, 1879
Married: Jun 1, 1900
Died: Jan 9, 1966

LaVerna Call
Born: Apr 1, 1881
Married: Jun 1, 1900
Died: Feb 2, 1968

Jacob "Roy" Chapin
Born: Apr 1, 1881
Married: Jun 12, 1902
Died: Oct 27, 1930

Mary Robinson Welshimer
Born: Nov 16, 1875
Married: Jun 12, 1902
Died: 1952

1st Cousins to Doris Marie
Mother's Side:
  James: Maxine, Merritt and Josephine
  Doris: Diane, Tom, and James
  Mary: Mary Francis, Smokey, Doug, Sandra and Marjorie
Father's Side:
  Phillip: Phyllis
  William: Roy and Mary JO

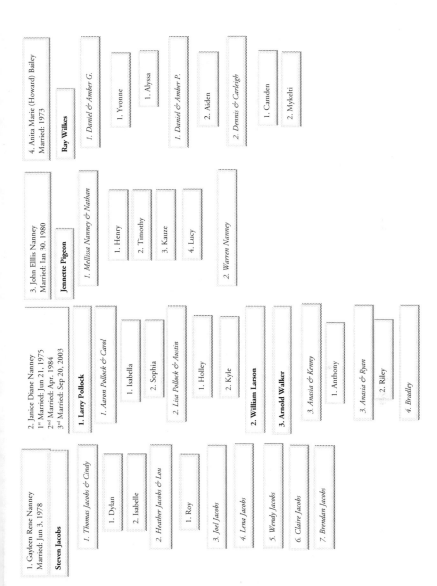

1. Gayleen Rene Nanney
Married: Jun 3, 1978

Steven Jacobs

1. Thomas Jacobs & Cindy
  1. Dylan
  2. Isabella
2. Heather Jacobs & Lou
  1. Roy
3. Joel Jacobs
4. Lena Jacobs
5. Wendy Jacobs
6. Claire Jacobs
7. Brendan Jacobs

2. Janice Diane Nanney
1st Married: Jun 21, 1975
2nd Married: Apr. 1984
3rd Married: Sep 20, 2003

1. Larry Pollock

1. Aaron Pollock & Carol
  1. Isabella
  2. Sophia
2. Lisa Pollock & Austin
  1. Holley
  2. Kyle

2. William Larson

3. Arnold Walker

3. Anasia & Kenny
  1. Anthony
3. Anasia & Ryan
  2. Riley
4. Bradley

3. John Ellis Nanney
Married: Jan 30. 1980

Jennette Pigeon

1. Mellissa Nanney & Nathan
  1. Henry
  2. Timothy
  3. Kauze
  4. Lucy
2. Warren Nanney

4. Anita Marie (Howard) Bailey
Married: 1973

Ray Wilkes

1. Daniel & Amber G.
  1. Yvonne
    1. Alyssa
1. Daniel & Amber P.
  2. Aiden
2. Dennis & Carleigh
  1. Camden
  2. Mykelti

TABLE OF CONTENTS

James Henry & LaVerna Andersen

It was August 19, 1879. The day was sunny, the sky clear and the mercury standing at 98 in the shade and no shade. The place was a wide place in the highway called Farmington, Utah.

This day turned out to be the greatest day in my life. I came into the world, an ugly, redfaced, snubnosed, bowlegged, bigmouthed, baldheaded, squacking baby, and have been squacking ever since. My mother in later years said I was a pretty baby and had a very good disposition, but I well remember that for the first six months of my babyhood she was ashamed to show me to her friends. The relatives, of course, had a chance to make my acquaintance, and I recall they told my mother I was a "sweet" kid, but as they turned away I frequently heard them remark: "What a homely little boy." I resented these unkind remarks until the first year of my life had passed, at which time I was first permitted to look into a mirror, and after that I no longer held a grudge against my relatives for their spontaneous remarks about my facial peculiarities. I really never knew the value of being what charitable folks call "plain looking" until I started my college career, since which time I have always been deeply grateful for those responsible for my physical looks. I found that I was not troubled by being pursued by a bevy of predatory females, as were the "sheiks" of my day, and consequently I had plenty of time to study and improve my mind and incidentally a little to spare, which I used in the valuable way of cooking up trouble for my more fortunate fellow students, whose minds run more freely to the adolescent walks of life.

James Henry Andersen

No "wide place in the road" has ever been able to hold me for long, and at an early age I found myself being transported in a covered wagon to the Cache Valley, known at the time as "Poverty Flat", which name, I understand, it has always lived up to. There I learned to tease toads, frogs, harmless snakes, and my brother and sisters. I also learned to milk cows, feed livestock, farm, and pull weeds, but I well remember that the effort to get me to do the work was worth as much as the labor performed by me.

Through the grade schools I went with a few whippings from the teacher each week. These were not usually for neglect of my school work but for fighting with other pupils and playing tricks on a few of the teachers, whom I regarded as being absolutely devoid of humor. They actually failed to see the funny side of my jokes even if the joke was on them. I usually passed my grades or was promoted, as 1 now recall, because the teachers desired to shift the responsibility for my decorum.

My principal occupation was fishing, hunting, and swimming, but none of these sports were permitted on Sundays, so I almost exhausted my repertoire of alibis keeping my skin unscathed after violating this rule. I recall once I had to explain why my shirt was on wrong side out on returning home Sunday evening. Quick thought impelled me to advise that it got turned as I was crawling through a wire fence. It was not the right answer.

My parents were long suffering and kind and in order to make something of me, strained every effort to raise the money to send me to the B. Y. C. at Logan where I completed my high school and two years of college work. I graduated in 1897 after carrying five majors and four minor subjects the last two semesters. That was where my social unpopularity redounded to my everlasting benefit. I believe I fully appreciated the sacrifice my parents were making to send me to school. It was a wonderful experience for me and changed my entire outlook on life. After graduation I was "called", (I think at the suggestion of my folks) to serve as a missionary, and for two years expounded, yelled, talked, and perhaps sometimes approached the point where it could be said with some degree of truth that I preached. I have no doubt that many persons were benefitted by my ecclesiastical efforts, though I have no definite proof that it was so.

I am now (1900 to 1902) installed in the school room where I teach the younger America the three R's and some other more or less useful knowledge, and during those three years, and specifically in July, 1900, I found a very fine and beautiful girl of about my own age, 1 seemed to be fooled by me into matrimony. Her name was Verna Call, and her home Bountiful, Utah. I think she fell in love

Doris Chapin Bailey

with my "beautiful character and lovable disposition," which she afterward found was more or less superficial. However, she was either game or too self willed to admit her mistake, because at this writing we are still well and happy, at any rate that seems to be the verdict of those who know us best.

I never could follow the ministry or school teaching. They both seem so necessary that the responsibility was too great for me. I have often thought that it was enough for me to be responsible for myself without being the keeper of the intelligence and ethics of the "ever so smart" children of doting parents, and the morals of the hypocritical community in general.

LaVerna Call Andersen

"Time wears on apace." Now I am in the mercantile business in Pocatello, A lamb among wolves. And when the Railroad strike of 1903 tied that town up as tight as a buckskin sack sewed up with a dog chain did the wolves eat me up? I worked for the Pacific Express Company at wages so small I had to get a magnifying glass to discover the bulge of the stomachs of my now growing family. My patience with children was not one of my best virtues even though, perhaps, I had few virtues of any kind worth recording. But it was not a virtue but a duty to feed my family, as I have ever realized, so I hired out to dig a basement. I worked almost half a day at that Job and was so disgusted I never called for pay#

but donated it to the Church, as it was a church basement that was being excavated; so I can actually, in my own mind at least, be credited with contributing something to the advancement of religion.

I now started reading law in the office of a good lawyer friend of mine, namely, Douglas Smith of Pocatello. I took a civil service examination and even though I dote not on exams I passed and procured a position in the Post Office at Pocatello, either as Cleric - or letter carrier. I preferred the outside job because it gave me more exercise and was a change from the work I was doing in the Law Office of Doug Smith.

Besides carrying letters, mowing a few lawns, studying law, and tending the baby boy part of the time, I had practically nothing to do; so I centered my I had had considerable railroad office training, particularly in rates and accounting and as the Government was advertising an examination for clerks with railroad experience for positions in the Interstate Commerce Commission 1 applied for, took, and strange as it may seem, passed sufficiently high rating to obtain the position.

This position, which I immediately accepted, enabled me to matriculate at the National University at Washington, where, by working, days, going to school and studying nights, I finally graduated with the class of 1908 and secured a "sheepskin" from the University which proclaimed to the world that I was "learned in the law" and conferred upon me the degree of Bachelor of Laws, designated by the letters L. L. B. Was I a happy chap? I thought I had the solar system and the earth was my special apple.

During all of these years of preparation, my wife was the cheerful urge to effort. We fought out the financial problems like Grant fought the war: "On these lines if it takes all summer," and it took plenty of summers and winters too. In the meantime we acquire a daughter and her stomach was as difficult to discover as were those of the balance of the family.

After graduation I secured transfer to the Land Division of the Interior Department where, after examination by the legal department of the Civil Service Commission. I landed a berth in the Field Division at Denver as Special Agent and Prosecutor for the General Land Office.

In this position in 1909 is where I first found out that all the law and procedure I knew would make a very small book, and what I did not know was beyond capacity of understanding. I appeared opposite the best legal talent in several states with the unspoken words of the Christian martyrs upon my lips, "We who are about to die. Oh Caesar, salute thee."

At one time in a small town in Colorado 1 tried a case with a smart lawyer of considerable experience, and while I did not win the case, I made the lawyer angry enough to challenge me to fistic - combat. Well I either had to fight or run, and as my legs are short I determined my best stance was to stand and take it. Result? I won this battle hands down; and body too part of the time, but still I won, and from thence on I felt I could "hold my own" with most any lawyer. Time has proven that to be only partially true, but I have the satisfaction to date (wait while I knock on wood) of "standing and taking it" as it came to me.

After serving over a year with the Land Department during which time I acquired confidence and a degree of the responsibility required of an attorney I started out in Blackfoot to conquer the world as the greatest lawyer of all time. As to how well I succeeded, you the reader, will have to be the judge, and I have had so much experience with Judges it will not even make a dent in my thick hide when you decide against me.

Practicing law in Idaho has been a great life for me. I like it. I work hard at it and enjoy the pleasant experiences while I endure the unpleasant ones. On the whole it is extremely interesting and absorbing. During my sojourn in Blackfoot I have held the following offices: Probate Judge, re-elected in 1912 and resigned to practice law; State Representative, Idaho Legislature 1931 Session.

I had frequently argued to the Court in construing a law what I deemed to be the intent of the legislature in passing the law, but after serving a term in the Idaho Legislature I came to the ultimate conclusion that the Idaho Legislature has no intent, a fact I had long suspected, Elected Mayor of Blackfoot in 1935 and re-elected in 1937, a position I have held with great credit to the Council and City Officers who do all of the work while I take the blame if any, and can I take it? And do I take it? It seems that public office, (a thing I do not crave) is fraught with many dangers, and while the path is never smooth, who wants to walk on a smooth surface? One might fall and strain his political ambitions.

During my stay in Blackfoot our family has increased by the addition of three more daughters, one of whom is unfortunately

Doris Chapin Bailey

deceased. Our children are all intelligent and have been well trained, the credit for which is due almost solely to their mother.

I have two small granddaughters. On the whole I am especially fond of grandchildren. One can play with them until one is tired and then turn them back to their mothers without a qualm of care or conscience.

I must now cease effort because I am getting ready for a fishing trip, and hence cannot be bothered with anything so unimportant as my life history.

Margaret Maria White
J.H. Andersen's Mother

Telephone 221
P. O. Box 3 4 8

J. H. Andersen
COUNSELOR AT LAW
Blackfoot, Idaho

CONTINUATION OF THE LIFE HISTORY
OF JAMES H. ANDERSEN, WRITTEN
BY HIMSELF DURING A LUCID
INTERVAL OF HIS DECLINING
YEARS. ON ACCOUNT OF HIS FAILING EYESIGHT
TYPOGRAPHICAL ERRORS CANNOT BE CORRECTS)
UNLESS THE READER CORRECTS THEM HIMSELF.

Chapter II

I wrote Chapter I in about 1938 and closed with the report that
I was going fishing and could not be bothered with any further
biography, I was Mayor of Blackfoot Idaho at the time and
was re-elected for a third term. I could never quite figure the
reason for re-electing me unless it was that the citizens liked my
overbearing administration of their municipal affairs, I refused to
run for a fourth term so the Governor in 1911 appointed me as a
member of the Board of Regents of the University of Idaho which
automatically made me a member of the State Board of Education.
This assignment I filled without special distinction and no pay for
a term of five years at which time I realized I was ageing and must
make some provision for my family in case of my decease, and also
a Democratic Governor had just been elected and I did not want to

give him the satisfaction of moving me over. I do not care for the removal but I did not want it to come from such a source.

In 1912 after the passage of the military draft law by Congress president Franklin D. Roosevelt appointed me APPEAL AGENT to represent both the Federal Draft Board and the Draftee in case he wanted to appeal to Washington from the decision of the draft Board to require his induction into the Armed Forces, This job carried no pay not even paper or stenographer's services, so I felt like the drafted soldiers only I did not have to be bossed around by an army officer and did not get any pay for my time and expenses, I represented a great many draftees and the Draft Board on many occasions from 1942 to 1946 when I was relieved

Telephone 221
P. O. Box 3 4 8

J. H. Andersen
COUNSELOR AT LAW
Blackfoot, Idaho

of my services and at the same time received a letter of commendation from President Roosevelt and a round bronze medal attached to a three color ribbon, which I have never displayed or worn. I think I will attach it to this history as a token of my thankfulness that I was able to contribute some service to the war effort in addition to lip service. All of the paying jobs, of course, were dished out to deserving Democrats, which in as it should have been in as much as the Administration was democratic,

I am now approaching my 8lst birthday and my 60th wedding anniversary and as usual my wife does the work and I loaf around and talk politics.

Our eldest daughter passed away in 1942 (her name Lena Weltha Andersen Chapin.) she and her husband had one daughter Doris Marie (Bunny to me) who is married and living at the present time in Needles, California and is the mother of three children who of course are our great grand children. Our other children are all married and have been for many years and have families of their own all of whom are smart and intelligent the credit for which on the Andersen side goes to their mother and grandmother as the case may be.

Doris Chapin Bailey

When Mrs and I arrived in Blackfoot to live there were two automobiles in Blackfoot and about four in the County. You could hear them chugging along for miles and teams of horses gave them the whole road and ran away wildly with their vehicle and driver over the fields and through the fences amid the loud cussing of the teamster and his passengers if any.

Telephone 221
P. O. Box 3 4 8

J. H. Andersen
COUNSELOR AT LAW
Blackfoot, Idaho

I was acting City Attorney and prepared the first ordinances for paving the streets with blacktop. The contractor called the mixture "bitchilithic or Warrenite" pavement. The local residents thought he was swearing and objected to the city council,

Things are quite different In this year 1960. For instance; speeding gas cars will strike you down while crossing the street, unless you are alert and agile. Snitching posts have been placed along the curb on the sidewalks and unless you contribute a lady policewoman will haul you off to the hoosegow. Cows no longer feed on the grass on main street, but I have heard that in the rural part of the city some sneaky business boys keep a few piggies under cover of an old time whisky still. You may not like whisky made in a pig pen, but during prohibition days pig pens were more valuable for stills than for pigs. The pigs roamed the streets on the outside.

Times change. You should have seen the old West before Television and Radio hit the air. Ranchers lived in peace and in neighborly hamlets and peace officers were seldom called to their offices and Indians were friendly and roved about on the hunting grounds with only now and then a violent act. Now the Television depicts the early West as a rootin tootin fightin killin orgy that never ended and never settled down.

Doris Chapin Bailey

The facts are that if the early settlers and cowboys had killed half as many as shown on television the West would still be populated only by Indians and a few crooked poker players.

Advertising has made changes along with everything else. It has been interesting to be in the West since the 1870's. Now according to

Telephone 221
P. O. Box 3 4 8

J. H. Andersen
COUNSELOR AT LAW
Blackfoot, Idaho

Advertising on TV, Radio and in the papers no dealer sells for profit. He just sells to "save you money". The more you buy the more you save. All you have to do is carry your savings to the Bank and deposit it in savings. Trouble is you bot [bought] on credit to start with and you pay on each article two dollars a week for the rest of your life or have the dealer repossess the merchandise. Again a common expression of the Advertiser is "You will have to hurry in first thing tomorrow as they are going fast and only a few left." What a sucker to believe that kind of statement. If the dealer had only a few and they were going fast why would he spend money to advertise them?

I have been accused of being a pessimist. Well perhaps to a very slight degree. For instance I never believed you could raise pumpkins without planting the seed, I never believed you could make good citizens of youngsters without seeing that they grew up doing some useful service and learning basically the three R's well to start with.

Well I guess I will let someone else write the final page of my history. Whoever writes it I hope will be charitable enough to say if it happens to be a fact, that "he died like a gentleman" and it would be rather nice if he lied a little and said it if the death was otherwise. I am against falsehoods you understand, but there may

Doris Chapin Bailey

be extenuating circumstances. As I have always said; "If you cannot win standing up you can at least claim success while you are lying on your back".

By the way, my grandfather was ALWAYS A GENTLE MAN! DCNB

The Hundred Year Stretch and Beyond
The People and Events Populating the Life of
Doris Marie Chapin Nanney Bailey

At least twice in the past thirty years I have described to my grandson Aaron what I consider to be a remarkable fact of personal history. If I stand with my arms outstretched and hold my right hand with my daughter Jan's left and she holds her right hand with Aaron's left and then my mother, Lena, holds my left hand with her right hand and my grandfather James Henry Andersen, her father, holds her left hand with his right hand, there will be 5 immediately related people standing in a row stretching one hundred years. My grandfather was born in 1879 to my left and my grandson was born in 1979 to my right. I find this fact starkly but exhilaratingly interesting from a number of different perspectives.

CHAPTER 1

The Andersen-Call Side

My great-grandfather Andersen's grandfather Andersen was born in Denmark and was a proselytized handcart Latter-Day-Saint (Mormon) who, as a child, walked to the "Promised Land" in Utah pushing/pulling a handcart. Grandpa was born August 19, 1879, in Farmington, Utah. My grandmother's father was Chester Call of the well-documented Mormon Anson Call family. I have been told that Chesterfield, Idaho, was named for Chester Call, one of Anson Call's sons. I have since learned that there is some controversy over the naming of Chesterfield. Therefore, I won't speculate further on the town's name. The town and Chester Call's house is currently being rehabilitated by people interested in saving its history. Chester was a twin, although I do not know the name of his sibling. Grandma was born April 1, 1881, in Bountiful, Utah. Both my grandparents were offspring of polygamous families and both were devout Mormons, married in the temple July 18, 1900, and married for almost 66 years.

My cousin Diane and I went to visit Chesterfield in 2012. I highly recommend a visit to family members. It was educational and inspiring and made the early days of Idaho and Utah come alive for me. Chester Call's house had many pieces in it that I recognized, having grown up with those pieces in Aunt Dot's home (Doris Andersen Smith).

My grandparents, James Henry Andersen and LaVerna Call Andersen, had five children. The oldest, my Uncle Jim, was the only son, born in 1901. He was the "rascal" of the family, and managed to get into trouble sufficiently on occasion that my grandpa had to bail him out. This information came to me via my dad so it is reasonable family history. This included either a marriage or a liaison with an "unsuitable" woman, who, according to my dad, Grandpa was able to pay off so that she "went away." Uncle Jim and Aunt Elsie, apparently a "more suitable woman," had three children: Maxine, Merritt and Josephine. Aunt Elsie was a very interesting lady. I always thought she was lots of fun because she loved to tease and tell jokes. Grandpa loved roast beef and was the one who always cooked the roast so it would "be cooked correctly." Grandma adhered strictly to the LDS stricture to "eat only a little meat." Aunt Elsie and Grandpa always had a teasing competition on their capabilities of cooking roast beef. She always said she made the best pot roast west of the Mississippi. Aunt Elsie's pot roast would be fork tender, falling-apart-well-done and delicious. Grandpa's would be medium rare, tender and out of this world. In my very young opinion, both were perfect. Grandma would only eat a tiny piece of Aunt Elsie's and none of Grandpa's.

My mother, Lena Weltha, was second, born in Pocatello in 1905. Margaret was born in 1911 and died in 1913. She and my mother both had diphtheria and scarlet fever simultaneously. Margaret perished, being too young to fend it off, this being prior to antibiotics. It left my mother with Bright's Disease. The term

Lena Weltha Andersen Cahpin

"Bright's Disease" is no longer used in the medical community since practitioners now know a great deal more about kidney function than they did in the first half of the 20th century. It is hard for me to determine exactly what this meant for my mother, other than nephritis and eventual kidney failure. On July 17th, 1938, my grandfather sent my grandmother and my mother to Mayo Clinic in Minnesota for a complete medical work up. I would have been four years old at the time. According to my mother's diary:

"Left home [Ketchum] for Blackfoot, then Rochester, Minnesota. Afraid I wouldn't return. Sad and blue but [it's the] only thing to do. Doctors there gave some help and started back August 2nd Mom and I. Sure much better and lots of hope for future. Glad to get home to Doris [Marie] in Blackfoot August 4th, then saw Ellis again August 6th and home August 7th. Boy what relief, how happy I am to be here"

The report to the family, however, was that the doctors were saying there was nothing they could do for her and she had about five years left. This information came from Aunt Dot. My mother died almost five years later on December 22, 1942, collapsing two days earlier in a uremic coma. She never regained consciousness. I was their only child, born ten years after they married, after she suffered several miscarriages, both before and after my birth.

Doris Andersen Smith

The last two of my Andersen grandparents' children were Doris, born in 1914, and Mary, born in 1920. I was named for Doris and was born two days after her twentieth birthday. She loved her sister Lena and her brother-in-law Ellis and frequently "ran away" in the summer to be with them. I knew Doris as Aunt Dot and she became one of the most important adults in my young life and one of the most important people in my entire life. She had Grandpa Andersen's sense of humor and loved to pull pranks and jokes on people along with having my Grandma Andersen's compassion and sense of appropriate behavior. She was a joyous and gracious and delightful person to be around, always quietly generous and hospitable. When my first grandchild was born she phoned Roy to ask how he was enjoying sleeping with a grandma. On the other hand, as her grandsons reported during the life sketch they gave at her funeral, she would write a thank you for a thank you letter. She was an incredible person who lived to the fullest until she was 97 years of age, and passed away on April 9th, 2011. She married her high school sweetheart, Thomas B. Smith, Jr., on June 21st, 1936. She chose that day because it was the longest day of the year and she wanted her wedding day to last as long as possible. I now own the two hand made and beautiful wedding gifts that my parents gave them. My mother made and sent them a lovely "postage stamp" quilt made from pieces of her house dresses. My dad's gift was to build a darling small cedar chest. Aunt Dot and Uncle Tom had three children, Diane LeVerna, born in 1937,

Thomas III, in 1939 and James "Jimmy" Andersen in 1946. Jimmy was killed in Vietnam, the first week he was there, after graduating from Officer's Candidate School. This was undoubtedly the most profound loss they ever experienced and they never truly recovered from it. Uncle Tom once said to me, "It (Jimmy's death) was useless. What was gained?"

Grandma A & Jimmy

Uncle Tom and Aunt Dot lived in a house that backed on the creamery that Tom's dad founded and operated until he gave up the creamery business and made the building into a garage and car lot and showroom called Blackfoot Motors. The elder Tom Smith managed Blackfoot Motors, followed by Uncle Tom and then Tom III, until after Uncle Tom's death in the 1990's when my cousin Tom sold the business. The house was moved to University Avenue shortly after World War II. Remodeling and landscaping led to the beautiful home they lived in the rest of their lives.

Mary Marjorie, the last Andersen child, was a loving and caring woman, very much like her mother, LeVerna Call Andersen. Mary died at the young age of 60 from lung cancer. Both my Andersen grandparents, my Uncle Jim and Aunt Mary died of lung cancer. Grandpa died in 1966 and Grandma in 1968. Mary and her husband Jay Peter Merkeley were married in the Mormon temple and had five children: Jay Peter, nicknamed "Smokey" by Grandpa,

Mary Frances, Sandy, Doug and Marjorie. Uncle Jay was on a mission for the Mormon church in Honolulu when Pearl Harbor was attacked. The hula doll in my doll collection came from Uncle Jay's time in Hawaii. They were married shortly after the war. Uncle Jay went to medical school in Long Island, New York. He had his residency in Shreveport, Louisiana, and then came home to Pocatello and opened his practice. They built a lovely home out in the country and raised Arabian horses for many years. I was very fond of Uncle Jay because he always treated me like such a grown-up, for instance, tucking my hand around and under his arm when walking down town. He would always play board and card games with me and loved to tease me. I was married and had my own family when their children were growing up so I never became quite as close to them as I was with the other cousins. Mary Frances has a sparkling wit and is a great tease and a quick study, reminding me greatly of Grandpa and Aunt Dot.

Front Row: Aunt Dot, Aunt Mary & Grandpa A.
Back: Uncle Jim, Aunt Elsie,
Uncle Jay & Grandma

About seven or eight years after his marriage, my grandfather decided he wanted to become a lawyer in order to better his life for his wife and children. Although it was quite unknown in that time, with a wife and two children, he made arrangements to "read for the law" in Washington, D. C. and obtained a job working in a government office. The first day he went to work, he was given a desk and a pile of paperwork to take care of. He finished the pile by noon and went to his supervisor to ask for more work. He was told that he should re-arrange his working habits because the amount of work he had been given was approximately what he would be given each day. So after that first day, Grandpa would come to work and divide his work into two equal piles. He would finish the first pile and then study til noon. When he returned from lunch, he concentrated on the second pile and then studied until he was finished for the day. In this manner he was able to complete his studies in two years and return to Pocatello, Idaho. In 1910, he bought a house in Blackfoot, moved his family there, and started his law practice. They lived at 321 Shilling Avenue, Blackfoot, from that time until their deaths in 1966 and 1968 respectively.

Grandpa Andersen had a long and distinguished career. He ran for the Idaho House of Representatives at a time when there was a plan afoot to disenfranchise the Mormons of Eastern Idaho. He served two terms and fulfilled his promise to put that idea down. He was elected mayor of Blackfoot for three consecutive terms and served as a judge for a period of time which earned him the title of "Judge Andersen" for the rest of his life.

Grandpa enjoyed joking with his neighbor, Mr. Olson, four houses down the same block where Grandma and Grandpa lived, about the various qualities of Danes versus Swedes. Grandpa and Mr. Olson spent so much time teasing one another and planning practical jokes, that it was impossible to determine the source of the various practical jokes that were played upon each one. Grandma and Grandpa could not countenance animals in the house and, they never allowed pets in their home. The neighbors, during my entire childhood and young adult life, gathered every summer in various back yards nightly taking turns as each yard contained a cinder block fireplace, visiting around each outdoor fireplace and a sampling of various wonderful desserts. This activity resulted in a wonderful sense of community, belonging and caring. Conversation was eclectic but kind, running from politics to weather. One year on Grandpa's birthday which was conveniently in August, he received, as a gift, a large dog kennel. He was told the dog would have to be coaxed out. So, being the good sport he always was, he got down on his hands and knees and started snapping his fingers and whistling to the "little doggie." The dog simply wouldn't come out. So Grandpa reached in, felt the dog's fur and pulled out a beautiful, soft stuffed dog. Everyone, including Grandpa, had a wonderful laugh. He was teased about that dog from that time on and it earned a place of honor in the living room.

Grandpa took complete care of Grandma. She never wrote a check or paid a bill and never knew how much money they had or what they owned. Grandpa arranged to have Uncle Tom Smith take care of her after his death. However, as often happens, Grandma turned out to have quite an independent streak. She insisted on receiving money to do some of the things she had always wanted to have done to the house that Grandpa had never done. Daddy chuckled about that and always said "The Judge married a strong woman."

After Grandpa retired, he moved a couple of pieces of his furniture from his law practice home to use. He loved to play solitaire and could frequently be found back at his office desk playing solitaire. He walked to town each and every day. He enjoyed this daily walk which he eventually made using a cane to help his sometimes faulty equilibrium. He was very proud of still having his own teeth and credited using a toothpick after every meal for that fact. During the time I lived with them, he always asked me questions about my day and any book I was reading, as well as encouraging me in my writing. One time my friend, Barbara Farnworth, and I wrote a story and Grandpa illustrated it with pictures he drew for us. I still have my copy of that book, one of my first "writings." Grandpa enjoyed writing himself. He was a prolific letter writer and wrote whimsical poetry about everyday things that happened. Many of those letters and poems can be found in the book I put together containing all his writings that could be found. He also enjoyed smoking big cigars, which possibly led to the frequent incidence of lung cancer in the family. Grandma called him Henry and I can hear her call him to this day, "Henry? Henry". One day Grandpa drove his car downtown and didn't see a brand new set of stop lights at the intersection until someone honked at him. He finished going through the red light and then parked the car immediately on the other side and called Uncle Tom saying, "Tom, I'm not going to drive any more. I just ran this damn new red light. Come pick this car up. I've left it right here." He never drove a car again.

Grandpa was the one who handed out nicknames. My mother was Tootles, I was Bunny, my cousin Merritt Andersen was Skeeter and Jay Peter Merkley became Smokey. The only one that is still called by Grandpa's nickname to this day is Smokey. Occasionally, I am Bunny to one of Grandma's relatives but "Doris Marie" seemed to be the name that has stuck with me even today with members of this side of my family.

Grandma's house was always spotless although I never remember being nervous about that. Her kitchen, especially, was established with RULES! She never had a dishwasher because she was sure they could never get her dishes as clean as she could. There was a specific order to doing dishes. One always washed the glasses first, scalding them with lots of boiling water for the rinse, then the dishes with the same rinsing procedure. These were wiped and put away. Then the silverware was disposed of in the same manner. Lastly the pots, pans and other utensils were done. Bowls and other items were washed as they were emptied and her kitchen was usually clean and presentable before a meal was served. Nothing could be washed or put into her kitchen sink except items connected with the preparation, serving and eating of food. Anything else requiring a sink had to go to the bathroom or basement sink.

All their lives, Grandma and Grandpa started out each day with half a lemon squeezed in a glass of water. Grandma would never allow "lunch meat" or "hot dogs" on her menu. She thought these "prepared" meats were unclean. Maybe she had read <u>The Jungle</u> by Upton Sinclair about the meat industry at the turn of the century and decided very quickly upon those rules. She loved "creamed" vegetables, especially wax beans. She was famous for her "burnt sugar cake" and her Christmas "fruitcake" which, given her religious views, never contained any alcohol. We ate lots of corn on the cob, snap beans, tomatoes, squash, watermelon, peas and wax and green beans from the garden. She seldom fixed a green salad since Grandpa always ridiculed green salad as "rabbit food."

Grandma always remembered Memorial Day which was called "Decoration Day" back then. Nobody back then ever bought flowers. We picked huge armfuls of whatever was in bloom then - lilacs, bleeding hearts, forsythia, dahlias, "flags" (iris and gladiolas) and peonies. We took a car full out to the cemetery and decorated all the family graves. Grandma always made sure we put flowers on Grandpa Chapin's grave and later on Grandma Chapin's grave too. The other special holiday I remember was a Mormon Church one, "Pioneer's Day," celebrating the founding of Salt Lake City and the migration of all the pioneers who came to the "Promised Land." This was where Brigham Young said "This is the place." Everyone always dressed up in long dresses and sunbonnets and there was a parade and picnics, etc. I remember it more than 4th of July celebrations as I was growing up because of living with Grandma and Grandpa in 1943 and 1944 and then spending so much time there every summer as I was growing up. I was twelve or so before I knew there were other churches besides the LDS - Latter Day Saints. The Mormons were so strong in Eastern Idaho they didn't put signs on their churches - if you saw a church you knew what it was.

All the years after Daddy and Elaine were married, Grandma and Grandpa sent me money in the fall for school clothes. That was always exciting to go out and very carefully spend the money. I don't remember ever getting clothes for Easter or other times. I just remember getting school clothes when I got money from Grandma and Grandpa. That annual gift was always a puzzle to me because Grandma and Grandpa had sent some money to Daddy shortly after he and Elaine were married. Elaine returned the money to them, telling them that Daddy and she were perfectly capable of taking care of me. I know about this because when I went to

Blackfoot the following summer for my summer visit, Grandma asked me, with tears in her eyes, why Elaine had returned the money to them. I had to tell her I didn't know and that I hadn't known anything about them having sent money. To Elaine's credit, she did everything possible to keep the relationship with my mother's family, however. I was very grateful on many occasions for that. Grandma never spoke about money again but her feelings had been badly hurt.

Chapter 2

The Chapin-Welsheimer Side

Roy & Mary Chapin with Ellis

On my father's side, my grandfather, Jacob Roy Chapin, was always referred to as Roy. He came from a large family in Kansas about whom I know very little. Roy was born in Minneapolis, Kansas, on April 1, 1881, the exact date my Grandma Andersen was born. Mary Robinson Welsheimer Chapin was born in Warrensburg, Missouri, on November 16, 1875, according to John's genealogy records. Her grave stone shows an 1874 birth. I would probably be inclined to go with the genealogy records as opposed to the grave stone but that is an intuitive decision and not based on any facts with which I am familiar.

Grandpa Chapin was a diabetic before the use of insulin to control diabetes. He died in 1930 from diabetic coma. He was only 51 years of age.

Grandma Chapin, Mary Robinson Welsheimer, was seven years older than Roy. They had three sons, my father, Ellis Lewis Chapin, born in 1903, Edgar Philip, (called Philip) born in 1906 and Jacob William (called Billy) born in 1917. My dad and his brother Phil were born in Kansas. Billy was born in Firth, Idaho. Unfortunately I heard no stories about their lives prior to my daddy and mama's marriage and very little afterwards so the record is scanty. What little I do know is recorded here.

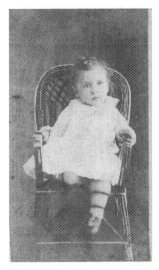

Roy Chapin

The move from Kansas to Idaho was part of a large migration northwest that seems extraordinary today. The railroad had established its rails across the continent and was, in 1909, the primary agent of the movement. Emigrants built a boxcar and loaded all their personal belongings as well as farm equipment and animals aboard. The railroad set the homemade boxcars onto special rails and the train set out with these cars, each of which was accompanied by members of each family represented. Roy Chapin and his six year old son, Ellis, went with their belongings, headed to a point near Shelley, Idaho, where Roy had acquired some farm land. Mary and 3-year-old Phil stayed in Kansas. They would make the journey later after Roy and Ellis got everything to their property and some kind of home ready to live in. Occasionally, one of the homemade boxcars would break apart, necessitating a stop of the train for a day or two while repairs were made. I have a postcard from Roy to Mary telling about one such stop they had to make. It also stopped every evening allowing people to get out, make a fire for a hot meal and sleep outside as well as take care of their animals. These emigrant trains, in the early part of the 20th century, were active for several years during the continued westward expansion of the United States.

What I know about Grandpa Chapin's death I learned from my mother's diary. Grandpa and Grandma Chapin and my parents were living in Stanley, Idaho, at the time. My Mother and Dad had a service station and a store and restaurant. Mother cooked for everyone who came to eat and my dad frequently took what seems to be tourists out hunting. I will quote from the diary as follows:

Mary Welsheimer

> October 1, 1930 - Wednesday - nice day. Got things ready for hunters – played pinochle till 1:30. Ellis got sleeping bag in and sold it right out.
>
> October 2, 1930 - Thursday - cooked, ironed dresses - served several lunches. Franklin from Twin

Roy Chapin

here until 1 a.m. Ruth & I went for swim, came back & fixed lunch.

October 3, 1930 - Friday. Fish for dinner. Franklin gave them to us – some fellows here all day waiting for some folks to bring their grub they forgot.

October 4, 1930 - Saturday - snow & rain. Lots of discouraged hunters - a good average of deer going out though.

October 5, 1930 - Sunday - snow - sold lots of chili, coffee and pie -

October 6, 1930 - Monday - snow. Franklins & friends stayed out on Sawtooths over night. One of the bunch was lost - they got a goat.

October 7, 1930 - Tuesday - snow and rain. A couple got lost in Bear Valley - after 3 days they found themselves and walked into camp.

October 8, 1930 - Wednesday - looks like it would clear up - hope so.

October 9, 1930 - Thursday - clearing some. Usual hunters coming & going.

October 10, 1930 - Friday - Ellis & Fred S, went hunting. I should say walking all day. Fairly busy at station.

October 11, 1930 - Saturday - had chicken dinner today - Bill & Jimmy lost in hills. We got excited that is Ellis & Phil didn't - boys found themselves and in ok. (This entry

Baby Ellis Chapin

refers to my mother's brother, Jimmy, and my dad's two brothers, Phil and Billy.)

October 12, 1930 - Sunday - Dull today wish it would hurry up and be time to close. Not enough business to keep open.

October 13, 1930 - Monday - Jason got here with dog & radio - look fine both dog and radio - I washed.

October 14, 1930 - Tuesday. Ellis went down to see father Chapin he sure isn't Improving - Bone's & new dog played "yelping hound blues" all night.

October `15, 1930 - Wednesday - made ice cream for Dad Chapin, he seemed to enjoy it but couldn't eat much.

October 16, 1930 - Thursday - snowed all night. Ellis guiding a hunter today - no luck.

October 17, 1930 - Friday - Dad Chapin worse. Decided to move down to cabin next to them so as to help.

October 18, 1930 - Saturday - Getting things ready to close up and move.

October 19, 1930 - Sunday - Dad Chapin sure sick. Not any business to speak of.

October 20, 1930 - Monday - started cleaning cabin & moved a few things down

October 21, 1930 - Tuesday - finished moving - will close station tomorrow.

October 22, 1930 - Wednesday - closed station and got cabin pretty well straightened up.

October 23, 1930 - Thursday - washed - sure tired but seems good to be here.

October 24, 1930 - Friday - Ellis has to help move his dad every little while - I'm afraid he can't last long –

October 25, 1930 - Saturday - I ironed & cooked - went up Chapin's but nothing anyone can do.

October 26, 1930 - Sunday - Dad Chapin seems to be unconscious part of time we sat up all night - Mrs. Wooly come over & sat with us - Also Glen V.

October 27, 1930 Monday - called Dr. Fox to come over from Hailey but nothing he could do. Dad Chapin died about noon. Ellis called Dad at Blackfoot. He sent car and undertaker.

October 28, 1930 - Tuesday - Phil, Bill, Mrs. Chapin & I got to Blackfoot 5 a.m. - went to bed. Ellis waited for car & came in with his father – made funeral arrangements.

October 29, 1930 - Wednesday - services today - lovely flowers – everyone lovely, especially Dad & Mother. We stayed in Blackfoot 2 weeks - Mrs. Chapin, Bill & Phil stayed Woodward's and Ellis & I stayed with folks and had a good visit before we went back to Stanley for the winter. And such a winter it will be. Stayed in Hailey overnight. Phil, Bill and Mrs. Chapin went show [movie]. We couldn't afford it.

November 9, 1930 - Sunday - Got Stanley noon - had dinner [at] Roses. Started getting settled again."

Mary Chapin was a teacher and played the piano for recreation. After her husband's death she lived between her sons Philip and Ellis. Eventually her allergies to orange blossoms became so severe that she was no longer able to live in California where Phil lived. When Daddy re-married after my mother's death, his new wife, Elaine Kitchin, was not aware of this arrangement and was unhappy with the idea of having her mother-in-law living with them. Grandma Chapin eventually moved to a home for the elderly

Phillip & Ellis Chapin

run by the Odd Fellows and Rebekkah's Lodge in Caldwell, Idaho. By that time we were living in Nampa, Idaho, and were able to have her come visit often. She also had a form of epilepsy which was spoken about in hushed tones within the family as "Grandma's spells." She would lose consciousness for a short period of time and didn't ever remember it when she recovered. Nobody had told me about this or given me any advice as to what to do, so one time when she did this when I was home with her by myself, I ran to the neighbors and brought them to the house to help. By the time we got there she had recovered and told them she was fine. No one ever knew (to my knowledge) whether her epilepsy was injury caused or genetic.

My new sister, Vicki Elaine, was born June 24, 1947. In 1948, she had what may have been an epileptic seizure. Elaine immediately took her to Salt Lake City and had a complete medical workup done to try to determine if she had epilepsy. I don't remember a great deal about this but I was told the tests

Billy Chapin

were positive and the doctors wanted to put Vicki on anti-seizure medication. Elaine declined and said she wanted to wait and watch her for a while first. Vicki never exhibited any symptoms after that time and never has taken any medication.

In 1951, the year I was a senior in high school, Grandma Chapin took a fall and broke her hip. It did not heal and gangrene set in. She died in 1952 just before my graduation and was buried in Blackfoot beside her husband. I remember a song she used to sing that I always thought was fun. The words were:

"Gee up and gee ho
Don't go so slow
T'will be night before you know it.
If you've got any spunk in your bones,
Now's the time to show it."

I also remember her crocheting. The beautiful

Grandma Chapin & Unknown Child

hand crocheted bedspread I have, she had crocheted for my mother as a Christmas present the year my mother died. Not too long after she finished it her eyesight began to fail and she stopped crocheting.

Grandma Chapin lived with us the first year Daddy and Elaine were married and then moved back to California with Philip and Helen. Philip was diagnosed with terminal cancer and Grandma came back to Idaho. She lived with us until she went into the Odd

Fellows Home. Phillip died in about 1948. Daddy and Elaine went back to California for his funeral.

My dad and mother and I went to California for a visit when I was very little, maybe five years of age. I remember seeing the pictures Daddy took of me on the beach on that trip but that's all. That is the only time I ever remember visiting Uncle Phil and Aunt Helen. I don't know anything about Aunt Helen at all, other than Daddy liked her and said she was good to Phil. That would have been approximately 1939 and was before Billy had married, although I believe he had joined the service. He was not in any of the pictures of that California trip.

Aunt Dolly, Uncle Billy's wife, was from Kentucky, was a fiery redhead and a WAC. When they married she was required to leave the service. Uncle Billy had fought in World War II, in the ski patrol. One of the big battles he was part of was the Battle of the Po River Valley in Italy. He received a battlefield promotion to Captain in that. He left the service after the war was over and tried chicken farming for a while in Southern California. He wasn't getting along very well trying to make a living, so he went back into the service and was sent to Occupied Japan. On June 25, 1950, the Korean War began and President Truman ordered troops to Korea. The troops in Japan were the closest available and immediately any officers who had been in World War II were conscripted to lead the green, non-combat experienced soldiers serving in Japan to a war zone. Uncle Billy was one of those officers and was killed within hours of landing on the Korean peninsula. I saw Aunt Dolly a couple of times when she came to visit after Uncle Billy's death, once in Boise and once several years later when she visited me in Capitola, California.

I had three cousins on that side of the family, but they were much younger and I never knew them. Phil and Helen didn't have children of their own and adopted a daughter, Phyllis. Billy and his wife Dolly had a daughter Mary Jo and a son Roy. Roy got pulled into the drug scene in California during the early years of the Vietnam War time and committed suicide. He came to visit Daddy and Elaine once in Nampa, Idaho.

I have often thought about the losses my Dad had during those few short years. My mother in December 1942, Uncle Phil in about 1946, Uncle Billy in 1950 and his mother in 1952. He never spoke to me about any of his family members after that time, especially my mother. Early after her death I tried to ask him questions but he would never answer and I quit bringing it up.

An interesting aside to the beginning of the Korean War happened at the Presbyterian Church camp I was attending on June 25, 1950. Every evening at camp we had a huge bonfire at the end of each day where we gathered and sang songs and had general camaraderie before going to bed. The fire was always prepared ahead for lighting early in the day. We had just received word of the start of the Korean War when the prepared fire spontaneously burst into flame, apparently from the fire the night before not having been extinguished completely. We went to the brightly burning bonfire a bit early that night, somewhat awed by the unplanned fire bursting out upon word of the fighting in Korea.

CHAPTER 3

The Early Years

Lena & her Bear Steaks

The Chapin family lived in several southeastern Idaho towns over the years. Uncle Jim, Ellis and Lena met and became friends in high school in Blackfoot. Ellis and Lena fell in love and on June 1, 1924, Ellis and Lena were married in the Andersen's living room. My mother was nineteen and my dad was twenty-one. Lena's parents had not wanted her to get married due to the Bright's Disease and the fact that pregnancy stressed a woman's kidneys. The doctors had discouraged thoughts of their having children. However, Lena was adamant that she wanted children and had many miscarriages trying to do so. She and Ellis would be married almost ten years before they were successful.

In the meantime, Lena's health was fragile and she was often ill and had to take to her bed. Her doctor suggested that perhaps the high altitude of the Salmon River country might help, so they moved to Stanley. During the summer they operated a small gas station and store and lived in a wooden-floored tent. Aunt Dot remembered at least two summers that she stayed with Ellis and Lena in Stanley.

When they were preparing to pack in for the winter to the cabin they occupied at Cape Horn, a lot of planning had to be done. The term "packing in" meant to literally pack all their groceries and supplies on horse's backs. Then leading or walking the horses by foot they usually went by snowshoes to their cabin. They had to take enough supplies to last at least six months when the snow was too deep for the horses to manage. They

Lena & her Dogs

had a small root cellar accessible from inside the house so the root vegetables could be stored without worrying about freezing. Otherwise, they used canned milk and lots of other canned foods, as well as copious amounts of flour, yeast, shortening and sugar for baked goods. The closest town with any doctor or medical assistance was Hailey, ninety miles away. They packed all their supplies for the winter to and into the cabin and then returned the horses to a lower elevation to spend the winter. Any kind of need during the time they were snowed in required the use of snowshoes and/or skis. Uncle Phil spent at least one, if not both, of the two winters with them. Roy and Mary Chapin, as well as Billy, had a cabin in Stanley. The only money earned during the winter was from the bounty the state had on cougar.

During one of the winters they stayed at Cape Horn, my dad got an abscessed tooth and had to snowshoe out to Hailey, living on aspirin. The tooth was surgically removed and he immediately started back to Cape Horn. My parents were strong people. My Uncle Jim told me one time that my mother was a superb shot and could always secure fresh meat for the table. He also mentioned that she was one of the first women who was prepared to go hunting in Yellowstone Park during the winter. Uncle Jim told me her aim was true and her knowledge of her weapon was substantial. Both my dad and mother had spent a good deal of time hunting in the Park so they knew the territory. They both loved the out of doors and spent a good deal of time hunting, fishing and exploring.

Ellis & Lena Chapin

My mother loved to tell the story about Daddy and his photography. One time in the middle of the night when they were camped outdoors, my mother felt a large animal drop from the trees onto her sleeping bag in the middle of the night. She whispered to Daddy, "Ellis, there is an animal on my sleeping bag." Daddy jumped up and took a flash picture, which frightened the animal away. It turned out to be a porcupine! She never let him live it down that his first thought was to take a picture of whatever it was, rather than save" her. One cougar hunt I remember my dad telling me about involved my dad and Uncle Phil tracking what they thought was one cougar and they had him treed. Uncle Phil shot the cougar which caused the second cougar they didn't know about to leap from a ledge and spread eagle Daddy into the snow. He couldn't move because the weight of the cat had driven his legs down into the snow. Uncle Phil couldn't shoot for fear of hitting Daddy and it was quite a scene for a while. I don't remember exactly how it was solved, but obviously it was solved, since Daddy was here to tell the story. Daddy said they later figured that the one cat had actually walked in the tracks of the other, which made it impossible to know there were two.

Daddy talked about driving a gas truck to Stanley over Galena Summit, which was an (almost) one lane dirt road over a very high mountain pass north of Ketchum. He always looked at the license plate of any car he met coming from the opposite direction. If it was an in-state car, he would get over as far as he could and let them go around him. If it was an out-of-state car, he would get out of the truck and ask them to let him drive the car around the truck. When I was a little girl I used to want to close my eyes when we drove that road, because the sides were so steep and the drop off so severe. Daddy used to tell me that if I closed my eyes he would have to close his, too, so I never was able to close my eyes, because he had to drive and to do that he had to keep his eyes open.

My dad had been given a camera as a teenager and he was immediately and totally smitten. He took a correspondence course in photography and taught himself how to develop his own film. There are notations in my mother's diary about the exams he took for that photography course and the studying. He experimented with light and shadow and was fascinated with how to take the best pictures in snow, shadow and with running water, such as fast moving rivers and streams and rapids and falls. He and his brothers enjoyed all the outdoor activity which Idaho had in abundance and learned to ski, snowshoe, fish and hunt in the wilderness. At one time, Idaho had the most wilderness area of any western state, with wilderness being described as area without any kind of road. What roads did exist in Idaho were unpaved and what cars were on those roads required frequent mechanical assistance, which young men in that day and age had learned how to do. A trip of more than a hundred miles required a great deal of time and preparation and plans for any contingency In many places, the roads were little more than wagon tracks, which had been molded by the weather and the sparse traffic. One such lengthy family trip was documented by my dad and the pictures recently found. This was before his marriage and he appears to be in his teens in the pictures.

Daddy continued to take pictures and, by trial and error, gained the technical experience he needed. He had an eye for composition and used the fascinating nuances of light and shadow to good effect, also learning how to take pictures of running water and snow. He had taught himself to tint pictures for color and taught my mother how to do so too. Soon he was being asked by people if his pictures could be purchased. His scenery pictures were especially beautiful and Idaho had many spectacular scenes to be recorded. He opened a photographic studio in Hailey and eked out a living for a short while. However, his forté was not portraiture but the great Idaho outdoors. That business failed and once again he operated a service station, which also had a few retail items for sale as well. I actually remember the penny candy, a large glass case with boxes of various kinds of candy, each piece for sale for one penny.

Trying to determine where my Dad and Mother lived in the ten years before I was born and up until 1937-38 when we moved to Ketchum, has been frustrating. There is very little hard data to use to pin things down. I know all the places they lived but not exact times nor even inexact times. They lived in Pocatello right after they got married. Daddy worked in a potato chip factory. They lived in Stanley and the Salmon River country for a long time. They had a service station, restaurant and store in Stanley. Daddy drove the gas truck over Galena from Hailey to re-supply the station, and they spent two winters at Cape Horn on the middle fork of the Salmon River. They had a portrait studio in Hailey, and a service station in Picabo. There are pictures in my baby book from Picabo so that residence had to at least partially take place after I was born. I had been told Daddy worked for the CCC, or Civil Conservation Corps as a cook, but in researching these depression era work programs, I found that the CCC was for unmarried men. They were married in 1924, so I am suspecting the CWA, which is mentioned in my mother's diary, as the organization that later family members called the CCC. The three depression era work programs did very similar types of work and differed by structure, funding and political message. The CWA from my mother's diary was the Civil Works Administration. It was replaced by the WPA, or Work Progress Administration. All these depression era works programs ran until World War II and were terminated because they were no longer needed, due to the strong job market available during the war. My mother's diary frequently refers to Daddy's being gone to "camp" to work throughout this period of time, as well as the CWA, and how difficult it was to be left alone for long periods of time.

Almost this entire time Daddy also had his photography as a second job and certainly was able to make some money from it. My mother learned to help with the pictures and especially learned to tint to add color to the black and white photos, which were all that were possible in that pre-Kodachrome day and age. It is very evident they lived from hand to mouth during those years and were very careful with every penny. Grandma and Grandpa (Andersen) sent boxes of food, especially at holidays and a check when they were able. They strongly expected their children, after marriage, to take care of themselves, however, and what help they sent was intended to be supplementary and not primary. Of course, there were never boxes of anything when they lived at Cape Horn.

Because of inexact information and because the ongoing story is mostly anecdotal, I will not try to date all of the activities noted herein. Reading through her diary for the weeks just prior to my birth was an interesting exercise. From word of mouth information I've received about her pregnancy and my arrival, she had a difficult pregnancy with a lot of edema and frequently albumen in her urine. She seldom mentions any discomfort in her diary, but it's possible to read between the lines. The entry on December 26th, 1933, for instance, reads: "Walked [to] town with Ellis, saw Doc. Fixed dinner, then Ellis finished dishes. Ellis studied lessons all day." On January 3rd, 1934, (her 29th birthday) she writes: "I was sure surprised and Ellis had a wonderful dinner, never had any idea all day. Ellis said he would fix a birthday dinner for me and boy was it a surprise when Julia and family came with a big cake." January 10th, "Ellis worked dark room all day goes to work [for] CWA Friday. I finished ironing. Sure have a lot of funny feelings. Made squash pie." January 12th Ellis worked out CWA camp. I stayed home & sewed etc., up late last night and didn't feel so good today. I just have to get my sleep." January 21st, "Ironed & Ellis worked dark room. Invited [to] Olmsteds for dinner, home early, felt bad all night." January 25th: "Had cramps & pain most of night. Doc said probably the baby was ready. Didn't take castor oil." January 29th: "Didn't sleep a wink all night, so when Ellis left for work I slept 2 hours. Sure tired all day, lots of movement." January 31st: "Ironed in morning - legs hurt and so didn't go for a walk, the days seem so long." February 5th: "Feel fair - Ellis working - took castor oil & was up all night. Sure wish things would hurry. Ellis is sure good." February 6th: "Some days one upset after another, Fox [her doctor] left without notice. Consulted Wright - [he] says Twin Falls tomorrow."

February 7th: "Blankinships drove us to Twin. Saw Doc - wants me under observation few days. Got room Rogerson [hotel]." February 10th: "Mother called before I was up. Had dinner [at] Franklins. Had cramps all day but feel fine. Doc says some improvement." February 13th: "Up early. Took taxi to hospital, took hypos all day. Had to sit in delivery room. Sure felt tough - nurse didn't know much." February 14th: "Had oil enema etc. - sure got weak. Doc let me go at noon - went hotel & left on 1:20 bus for Blackfoot."

Beginning the following day her diary is written in my dad's handwriting not hers. February 15th: "Got home.......... Saw Dr. Beck. Everything OK. Went to bed early." February 17th: "Doris

(Mama's sister) came home from school. Dr. Beck asked me to be at hospital tomorrow night." February 18th: "Doris' birthday. Had nice dinner and drove Doris Pocy (- pronounced Pokey - nickname for Pocatello). Then went up to hospital." February 19th: "Had 17 shots Petriritrine and pains started in earnest. Ellis & Mother with me all night - Hard night." February 20th: "Baby Doris Marie arrived 7:45 a.m. Weighs 7 lbs. Dark hair, blue eyes and perfect. Everyone feels better. Sent announcements."

After struggling with the spelling of the medication; I have no idea what the medication is that she names. It appears to be something to induce labor, but I'm guessing. Her handwriting starts again on February 26th. Ellis had to leave her to go back to work on the 27th. She commented that she hoped "he wouldn't be too lonesome" and that she was "lonesome but guess I'll get used to it."

On March 2nd, still in the hospital, she writes: "Got ready to come home - left hospital 1:30 - Dad carried me down stairs - went right to bed but got up for supper."

A few passages about moving and money lead to more knowledge about what life was like for them. On April 24, 1934, my mother writes: "Ellis got job [in] Gannett & left - don't know how or when he will be back." He was back home the following day. On May 4th, 1934, she writes: "Ellis can't get in any shifts in Carey, costs more trying to work than wages pay."

And so the struggle to make a living continued but her diary indicates happiness with their marriage and with the new member of their little family.

CHAPTER 4

Ups and Downs

We lived in Picabo where I remember the gas station with the penny candy for sale. In looking at my baby book we had a beautiful big dog that I loved. A good deal of time was spent enjoying their long-awaited child. My mother continued to yearn for a second child and apparently was pregnant again for a sufficient amount of time that she noted the name of Dorothy being expected to be coming for a sister. They were both ecstatic. However, other than that one cryptic comment no other mention was ever made. The only comment my dear Aunt Doris ever made to me was that my mother had "numerous miscarriages both before and after my birth."

Union Pacific Railroad had decided to build a ski resort outside the tiny town of Ketchum. At that time Ketchum was known as the place where sheep were gathered to be shipped to market in the fall. There were a large number of Basque sheepherders who had migrated to Idaho to take care of the large number of herds. They lived in covered wagons out with the sheep all year long. There was lots of grazing ground good for sheep in those Idaho hills. Sheep and cattle don't co-mingle well because sheep, when grazing, pull the grass from the roots and a considerable time is needed before that land can be grazed again. Cattle clip the grass to the ground and it grows back more quickly. There were many armed flare-ups that occurred in the years around the turn of the century between the cattle people and the sheep people. The sheep that were being kept for breeding were sheared and then taken back out to lower elevation winter grazing grounds. The lambs were sent to market.

In 1935, Averell Harriman, head of the Union Pacific Railroad, was brainstorming to come up with ideas to market the West to the public as a place to come visit. He was an avid skier himself and was hoping to find a special place to build a ski resort. He hired a young European Count, Felix Schaffgotsch, to travel, around the Western states to find a spot that reminded him of Austria and the Alps. He passed up areas like Aspen which he felt just didn't have the right "feel." Tipped off to a place very far removed from that day's vacation spots and essentially isolated but surrounded by magnificent mountains of various steepness and forest, Ketchum was "discovered." The Count raved to Mr. Harriman about finding the ambience of the Austrian Alps and was soon joined by Mr. Harriman who became as taken with the area as the Count had become. Ketchum, a lonely mining and sheep shipping town was soon to become a bustling community of construction and a quest for something unique and as European in aura as possible. Harriman hired Steve Hannagan, a public relations specialist, with success on his résumé listed as the transformation of a sand dune into Miami Beach. In nine months, Sun Valley was named Sun Valley by Hannagan and opened its doors at a cost of 1.5 million dollars. The gala opening in 1936 was attended by such movie stars as Clarke Gable and Erroll Flynn. It was ready made for a photographer who knew the country and had already mastered the reflection and light problems of moving water and bright sun on snow.

My dad was very much aware that he was going to have to promote himself since he was totally unknown to the powerful cadre of people financing and building Sun Valley. Exactly how he garnered attention from Steve Hannagan, I have no idea. However, family word of mouth and a few comments in my mother's diary indicate that he took large numbers of pictures of Sun Valley and its celebrity guests and got those pictures to Mr. Hannagan's eye. To my biased mind, in addition, it had to be obvious that hiring the photographer who made such spectacular pictures and got along so well with the celebrities, as well as had the experience and knowledge to entertain those celebrities with real hunting and fishing trips, would be much less expensive than buying individual or contracted pictures. By 1937, Mr. Hannagan was sold on Ellis Chapin who had acquired the nickname by which he would be known the remainder of his life, "Chape." The little Chapin family moved from Picabo to Ketchum.

The first little house we lived in was owned by some people by the name of Fatig. Then we moved to a big house with living quarters on each side. They didn't call them duplexes back then, but that's what it was. A family by the name of Chamberlain lived on the other side of us. They had twin boys, Dee and Craig, and I promptly fell in love with Craig. They were the same age as I was. There were half a dozen or more kids who played together. We loved to play cops and robbers and built a lot of forts using old lumber and branches, which we used to fasten old blankets or whatever we could find to make an enclosure. I managed to lose a few fingernails to falling boards during the construction of these "hideouts. Sometimes we constructed a stage, invented a story line and had costumes and dialogue. We then invited all the grownups to attend for a penny apiece.

One time there was a Sun Valley party for all the kids at the Christiana Club. It was a very elegant restaurant and gambling place for adults. My dad's connection to Sun Valley gave me an invitation to this very exclusive children's event. I remember my mama spent a lot of time and effort fixing my hair and getting me dressed up. I don't remember anything about the event itself, but when we were taken home, I was dropped off at the curve of the road where our house was located. There was a huge mud puddle right there and since it was dark I didn't see it. I tripped and fell into the muddy water getting my beautiful clothes and shoes and stockings all wet and muddy. I cried all the way home. Actually, I cried a considerable amount. I was a well-spoiled girl.

I also remember my 6th birthday party, which Daddy arranged for me at Trail Creek Cabin. It was a secluded and exclusive clubhouse that was used as an Officers Club during the war and as a special place for private parties otherwise. I will never forget my birthday cake that year. The Sun Valley chef made it in the shape of a mountain with trees and skiers going down the sides. It was very exciting and the most wonderful party I had ever had.

My daddy and mama loved to take walks together and in the spring Mama always wanted to go see the spring wild flowers. Her favorite was the columbine. In the fall the goldenrod always gave Daddy hay fever but we would go out to see it and see the Indian Paint

Brush, which was so plentiful. Mama loved sweet peas and always planted a long row of them to use for inside bouquets during the summer.

After Pearl Harbor was attacked and we were at war it seemed like everything was rationed and I was constantly being reminded to be careful of things. We could no longer take long drives because gas and tires were rationed. We saved scrap rubber and metal; I remember dragging a pair of rubber hip boots down to the service station, which collected all the things being saved for the war effort.

When I started school (first grade, there was no kindergarten) my mother and I walked to school. The school was fairly new and there were four school rooms, each room was for two grades. When you got to high school age you had to take the bus to Hailey, as Ketchum didn't have a high school. There were ten to twelve students in each room and I don't ever remember there being a difference between the two grades in that room. I do remember learning the Palmer method of handwriting and thought the writing exercises were a lot of fun. Since I loved school I was successful in it and enjoyed praise for my penmanship, spelling and reading. When the war started I remember buying war stamps, which were smaller donations than war bonds, which were sold to help finance the war. These stamps were pasted into a little book. The stamps were 10 cents apiece and when you had collected $18.75 they could be turned in for a bond. Essentially the purchase of stamps and bonds were loans to the federal government for the war effort. Millions of dollars were raised via this method, which allowed the manufacture of war goods so that our soldiers were as well-equipped as possible.

The other thing I remember about school is that is where I suddenly started fainting. I have no idea what triggered it, but I fainted once or twice a year clear into my twenties and then suddenly stopped. I did learn the symptoms, however, and in my older teen years was able to get my head down between my knees until the feeling passed and I was okay. The first time it happened an older student was sent to my house to get my mother, who had to walk to the school to get me. I always felt really bad about her having to do that and was glad they never called her again. I was protective of my mama because she had terrible health problems and I was always told I had to be good to help her, so I tried to do that.

Ernest Hemingway, by all accounts, was completely taken by the Sun Valley area and, beginning early in the history of Sun Valley, came annually to hide away to write. My dad always told us that Hemingway wrote <u>For Whom the Bell Tolls</u> during those first years that Sun Valley was open, hiding away with nobody knowing he was there, and taking short and happy fishing trips with my dad as a break from his writing. Hemingway was what was called "a man's man." He and Gary Cooper were two of a kind and became very close friends. The two came each year to hunt and fish together in the wilderness areas of central Idaho. Daddy enjoyed that kind of living with a passion and frequently was the "guide" who took them on their next adventure. Daddy enjoyed regaling them with stories about a deep canyon where the pigeons were very difficult to shoot because of the wind currents. After many stories and suggested bets, Ernie, who was an expert marksman and proud of it, asked Chape to take him there. So Daddy was able to introduce Ernie to Malad Canyon, a deep short canyon on the Snake River south and east of Sun Valley. Ernie used up four boxes of shells and finally got four pigeons. It was a huge blow to him to take such a long time to hit his target but he was such a good sport and was actually extremely pleased that my dad had been able to find a place that proved to be such a challenge to his prowess. After the Malad Canyon experience, Ernie usually asked for Chape to be his guide for the fishing and hunting trips.

My dad had a repertoire of stories about the famous people with whom he mingled and whose pictures he was being paid to take for publicity for Sun Valley. The first important person he ever photographed was Ethel DuPont. She wanted to go hunting. It was winter and she did not like reporters. Chape took her hunting in Shoshone and she "had the best time of her life." This was the beginning of my dad's reputation.

Hemingway had three sons when Daddy first met him: Jack, age 17, "Mousie" Patrick, age 13 and "Giggy" Gregory, age 8. When Giggy was about nine years old he shot craps with some friends and won $80. He wanted to stop playing, but Ernie made him go back and play some more because he was playing with friends. Ernie told him that if you go downtown and gamble with strangers and are $80 ahead then you can quit, but not when you're playing with friends.

Ann Roosevelt came out to Sun Valley and was totally bored with everything. Daddy decided he would take her down to Shoshone to shoot rabbits. The state was paying a premium to have people come and shoot the rabbits because farmers were losing their crops. She could not get over the thousands of rabbits that were overrunning everything in sight. Then she would cuss and swear because the rabbits she was shooting would not stand still. After all was said and done she proclaimed she'd "never had a better time."

Daddy knew Bing Crosby quite well too. He was a very different person from Ernie. I remember going sleigh riding with Crosby's sons one time. Bing enjoyed the fishing and hunting but not as much as Cooper and Hemingway. Cooper and Hemingway could spend hours telling stories from all over the world. Crosby was not as much of an outdoorsman as they were.

The 1936-39 Spanish Civil War was of large importance to the Hollywood crowd. Ernest Hemingway had gone to Spain because he had received word that his son, who had gone to Spain to volunteer with the Loyalists, had been captured. While in Spain trying to find his son, Ernie had gotten his knee shot up. Robert Capa's wife, Gerda, was there as a war photographer, along with Hemingway. There were planes shooting at the convoy they were in and the driver of the car was hit, causing the car to veer into the convoy, killing Capa's wife, who was hanging off of the running board shooting pictures. Ernie grabbed Capa's wife's camera and handed it to Capa, telling him to start taking pictures because he (Ernie) knew nothing about cameras. Capa became well-known for his war photography. Robert Capa was actually a fictitious name. His real name was Endre Erno Friedmann, a Hungarian, with a fascinating life story. Among many online accounts is: http://www.pbs.org/wnet/americanmasters/episodes/robert-capa/in-love-and-war/47/

We moved into a beautiful house in the fall of 1941. I remember how excited Mama was and how beautiful the house was. I had an upstairs bedroom and when we first moved there it was strange and a bit scary to me because I had always slept closer to Mama and Daddy. I remember my Mama coming upstairs to sing a lullaby to me those first few nights. It was a song she often sang to me:

Sweet and Low
Sweet and low
Wind of the western sea
Low, low, breath and blow,
Wind of the western sea.

Over the rolling waters go
Come from the dying moon and low
Daddy will come to thee soon.
Sleep my little one.
Sleep my pretty one.
Sleep.

I will always think of my mother when I hear this beautiful song.

I was with my parents in Sun Valley when Pearl Harbor was attacked. It was a somber and terrible time for a little girl of not quite eight who was frightened because she didn't understand at all what was happening and the reactions of the adults around were terrifying. Within a year, the scene at Sun Valley was completely changed and the Union Pacific Railroad closed the resort to the public. The United States Navy took over the site as a rehabilitation hospital for their war wounded who were coming back from the

South Pacific. They needed medical facilities closer to the West Coast for servicemen in need of rehabilitative services. Steve Hannagan had connections with Ford Auto Company and with his assistance my dad was supposed to proceed to Detroit to start taking pictures to help the war effort. We packed up and left Sun Valley just before Christmas in 1942 with the plan to go to Blackfoot and have the holiday with the family. Then we would be going by train somewhere east where Hannagan had arranged for Daddy to work for Ford Motor Company taking pictures. Sun Valley was closing "for the duration." We reached my grandparents' house in the early evening on the 20th of December. The house was all decorated with holiday lights. Aunt Mary had painted a beautiful holiday scene on the front window.

Daddy, Mama and I ran up the stairs and into the house. My mother clapped her hands and said "Oh, everything is so pretty." She then collapsed on the floor. My dad ran and picked her up and laid her on the couch and someone ran and called the doctor. He came in such a hurry that his shoes were untied. She was put in the middle bedroom and my dad never left her side. The one time I was allowed to go in and see her I remember asking her how she was doing. I have sworn for years that she answered "better". However, all reports since I have become an adult indicate that she never regained consciousness. I was in the living room when she died and I heard my dad exclaim, "Lena!" He started sobbing huge, breath taking sobs that racked his body.

Everything was chaotic and totally foreign. I simply don't remember much of what happened in the next few days. I remember my mother being in a casket, which was put in Grandma and Grandpa Andersen's living room and what seemed like hundreds of people coming to "pay their respects." I remember being given some of the Christmas gifts that had been under the tree for my mother. One of these was the gorgeous hand-crocheted bedspread from Grandma Chapin. I still have this beautiful spread and I think of my mother any time I see it.

With my mother's death, obviously the plans were changed. It was decided that I would stay and live with my grandparents while Daddy proceeded to the job that was waiting for him. He was to take pictures of every part that went into making various war machines, from a tank on down. These pictures would be placed in books showing exactly how each piece attached to its immediate contiguous parts. These pictures would be put with a small amount of narrative into a book and shipped with all the parts so that the item could be put together and used at the scene by untrained persons.

Daddy left in early January on the train. I remember going to the train station and waving good-bye to my dad when he left to "go back East." Over the years I have been able to piece together the comings and goings fairly well. Daddy's first job was in Detroit. He was there during some major race riots. The only information I have on this period of time are some letters Daddy wrote to me. Almost every letter contained an admonishment to take care of my shoes because they were rationed and I couldn't get new ones easily. From Detroit, he went to Aberdeen Proving Grounds near Baltimore, Maryland. He was only away from Idaho for ten or eleven months in 1943. Sun Valley was being turned over to the U.S. Navy for a rehabilitation hospital and Hannagan called Daddy back to Ketchum and Sun Valley to do some publicity photography highlighting the Navy presence at the resort. I finished 3rd grade in Blackfoot after my mother died and also my entire 4th grade living with my grandparents.

When I first went to school in Blackfoot after the Christmas holidays, I remember Grandma and another woman and I walking up the stairs into the school. Something was said about how sad it was that I didn't have a mother. I was very unhappy about that conversation. It is interesting to me that I remember not being happy about that overheard conversation, but I don't remember exactly why. Grandma and Grandpa managed with my presence and I finished 3rd grade with no problem. I made friends with the girl who lived right straight across the street from Grandma and Grandpa. She and I became inseparable friends. That was back when Shilling Avenue had a median of grass in the middle of the street. We would run across the street and meet in the middle, dropping and rolling on the grass and giggling as only little girls can do. My friend, Barbara Farnworth, and I stayed in touch; she came to my first wedding, and we would see each other on occasion when I was in Blackfoot visiting Aunt Dot.

The summer of 1943 I went by train with Aunt Mary to Chicago, where Daddy met us and took me in hand. The train ride was very exciting to me, with the porters making up the sleeping bunks, eating meals in the dining car or buying food items from a black man who came through the cars at lunch time with a vending cart. This was my first experience with people of color, although, frankly, I didn't pay a lot of attention to things like that. I was given my own money for buying lunch and remember trying to tip the vendor but was quickly told that was inappropriate. I had wondered why he kept giving me the tip back.

I never knew why Aunt Mary was going back east but I went with my dad from Chicago to the boat docks, where we took an overnight ferry on Lake Erie. I do remember the ferry trip but nothing else about the trip to New York City. We stayed in the Hotel Statler, which appears to have an interesting history when looked up on the web. I distinctly remember the Hotel Statler in New York City. However, online research indicates only Hotel Pennsylvania in New York City. That hotel did not become the Statler Hotel until 1948. A nine-year-old's memory is not reliable, so I am obviously thinking the memory of the Statler Hotel comes from a stay in Buffalo or hearing about a stay in Buffalo, which could have coincided with my trip back to New York that summer. I remember being in Buffalo, although we did not go to the Niagara Falls. I remember the train trip and the overnight ferry trip, with the next complete memory being in a hotel in New York City where I spent a good deal of time in the beauty salon making a nuisance of myself. I remember having a good deal of time playing in that beauty salon and watching all the various procedures and hairdos. The advent of permanents had occurred recently and the equipment and chemicals used would be frightening today. However, it was exciting to women who were thrilled to be able to have curly hair "permanently."

I remember going to the top of the Empire State Building, an amazing thing to me, a young girl from Idaho where I hadn't ever seen buildings more than two or three stories high. We went to see the Statue of Liberty. I was disappointed because the stairway to the torch was closed "for the duration." That term was spotted frequently with regard to things which were postponed or cancelled until the end of the war. No one could buy a car, for instance, without a special permit, and if you had a car, gas was rationed as well as tires, if you could even get them. We did take the street cars, changing cars a couple of times, and went out to Coney Island. That was a wonderful adventure resulting in my first and last ride on a roller coaster. Daddy thought he was taking us on the "little" roller coaster! The rest of the Coney Island trip was fun, although we did get lost getting there and many things were "closed for the duration."

While we were in Baltimore we also went on a train to Washington, D.C. where we visited Aunt Alta and her family, some relatives of my mother's. The only other time I remember hearing about Alta was in the journal Grandma Andersen kept of a trip she took back to Washington, D.C. several years before. I do not remember the trip back to Idaho. I continued to live with my grandparents during 4th grade. I remember the awe that the family expressed when my Dad came to Blackfoot from "back east" with a brand new Ford car. No one had seen a new car since the war had started. In February, according to Elaine, my dad moved back to Ketchum (I believe it was actually right before Christmas) and when school was out in Blackfoot, I went to Ketchum to be with him for the summer of 1944. We lived at the Brandt's Cabins and Hot Springs in Ketchum.

Daddy had a lady friend come out from Detroit to visit him that summer. Her name was Esther Skoog. She was a school teacher and I remember liking her a lot. She taught me the trick of adding 9's whereby you decrease by 1 the number you are adding to 9 and add 10. The concept of math was difficult for me and I was thrilled with this help because I was determined to always have good grades. She and I spent a lot of time together visiting and I finally asked her if she was going to marry my daddy. Her face got very soft and she answered me very seriously that she had considered it for quite some time, but that she had always lived in the east and she didn't think she would be comfortable or happy living in the west. She had always been a "city girl" and Daddy was definitely one who loved the outdoors and wilderness. She cared for him greatly but, no, she probably was not going to marry him. She left very shortly afterwards and as the summer came to its end, I, too, packed up and went back to Grandma and Grandpa's. I hadn't been back at my grandparents for very long before we received the telephone call about my dad getting married. Grandma was very happy for me and gave me many reassurances that this was wonderful. I am sure that it was a tremendous relief to my grandparents to have me back with parents to take care of me. I never ever felt unloved, but at their age having a young granddaughter who needed a home had to have been difficult.

CHAPTER 5

My New Mother

Elaine Kitchin Chapin

I spent the summer with my dad at Brandt's Hot Springs in Ketchum between the 4th and 5th grades. It had been a fun summer, spent mostly in the swimming pool and included being brave enough to jump off the high diving board as well as nursing an ear infection. It had also included the visit by Esther Skoog from Detroit. It was mid to late August and I was entering the 5th grade at Blackfoot Elementary School. Grandma got the phone call. When I came inside from playing out in the yard, she greeted me with "You're going to have a new mother! Isn't that wonderful?" So I was packed up and returned to Ketchum to live with my dad and my new mother. My dad and Elaine Miriam Kitchin were married on September 30, 1944. None of her family were present. The commanding officer at Sun Valley walked her down the aisle in the theater at the resort.

Daddy always said their honeymoon was a camping trip to Dagger Falls, which Elaine had heard about from Navy officers who had gone there with Daddy. They had to walk in about ten miles, crossing creeks and climbing the steep terrain. Over on a hillside, Daddy pointed out a large group of coyotes jumping and catching grasshoppers, a special treat for the coyotes, who found them delicious. As they followed the small stream uphill Elaine was entranced with the presence of salmon going upstream to spawn. Daddy carried their sleeping bags and all his camera equipment and she carried the frying pans and a few potatoes. She also carried a fresh lemon to quench her thirst because she refused to drink any of the water from any of the creeks. The first night on their way, Daddy said, "Elaine, watch up there in that tree! Watch this stick I have in my hand." He made the stick roll through the air and right around a large bird's neck up in the tree, and it dropped to the ground dead. It was a grouse which Daddy immediately prepared for their dinner that night. Elaine did not remember him ever cooking again after that honeymoon trip, although there was frequent mention of him cooking in my mother's diary, as well as a family memory of him working as a cook for the CWA. At Dagger Falls he caught a salmon over fifty pounds in weight, which thrilled my dad no end. I heard many times from Daddy the story of catching that fish and how excited he had been. They ate the salmon while they were camped at Dagger Falls. Elaine was very spooked by all the small animals scurrying about all night and was glad they both fit in the sleeping bag because she was so afraid. In her notes, she indicated fresh admiration for my mother living out in the wilderness with Daddy in the Salmon River country.

After returning from Dagger Falls they went back to Chicago to introduce Daddy to Elaine's family. They arranged to have a friend named Eulalia watch me so I could go to school when they took the trip. They were gone two weeks. Elaine told me that I went all over Ketchum telling everyone that I was going to have a new baby sister. I suspect that was part of the bait my grandmother told me to make the marriage attractive to me. They also brought a large number of new clothes for me from Chicago. I'm afraid I was not very appreciative since my clothes, up to that time, had been mostly handmade and clothing from Chicago struck me as "uppity".

My "new mother" was Elaine Miriam Kitchin, who was from Chicago. It was only many years later that I learned she had grown up in Philadelphia. She was a Navy nurse at Sun Valley, which had been taken over by the United States Navy as a rehabilitation hospital and she had been in Sun Valley for about eight or nine months. She had first come to Sun Valley from Farragut Naval Training Station near Coeur d'lene, Idaho, on Lake Pend Oreille. As a trained registered nurse, she received officer's credentials and was a Lieutenant Junior Grade. A good description of Farragut is told by Marianne Love in the Sandpoint Magazine.

'It served as a small slice of life's big picture and ignited like a field of tinder dry weeds. It faded so quickly, like a wisp of smoke.

"Yet in spite of its momentary flutter, the sights, sounds and memories of Farragut Naval Training Station at the southern tip of Lake Pend Oreille flame within the hearts and minds of thousands of World War II veterans as if they happened yesterday. Its embers floated far from Farragut's boundaries, sparking nearby communities into an era of excitement and new blood. These days, cracked cement foundations, the brig, a few pump houses and two giant water towers have survived as the few visible vestiges of an era when the urgency of the war effort thrust North Idaho into a vital role.

"Farragut Naval Base rose almost overnight on wide-open fields and rolling hills that had once served as a seasonal stop for early Indian and pioneer migrations. In late 1941, the U.S. government snapped up the land from private owners, Kootenai County, and a railway company to establish an inland naval base more than 300 miles away from the western coastline, where the nation feared a Japanese invasion. For the next nine months more than 22,000 men worked 10-hour shifts for 13 of every 14 days for Walter Butler Construction Co. to build mess halls, libraries, movie theaters, living quarters, chapels and other buildings. In the great hurry and with a supply crunch, many of the 776 buildings were constructed with green wood. The flurry of construction activity provided a giant economic shot-in-the-arm for surrounding communities like Sandpoint, still mired in a slow revival from the Great Depression of the 1930s.

"They paid $1.60 an hour," recalls Hope resident Fred Kennedy, who later operated a tugboat/barge service on Lake Pend Oreille. "No one had ever heard of such wages." Carpenters, laborers and trades people from throughout the Sandpoint area pounded nails, hauled supplies and filled in wherever needed as the huge base sped into motion.

"Between its opening in September, 1942, and its decommissioning in June, 1946, this stunning expanse of 4,000 acres served as temporary home to almost 300,000 naval recruits. Located about 30 miles from Sandpoint at the far end of the lake, the Farragut Naval Training Station -- briefly to become Idaho's largest city -- served as boot camp for "Blue Jackets." During basic training, recruits left home for the first time, came to Farragut and learned to how march, row, swim and use firearms before heading off to the Mediterranean Sea or the South Pacific. Others received additional training as signalman's gunner's mates, the hospital corps or radiomen. WAVES (women naval officers) served as nurses at the base hospital."

I am not positive when Elaine arrived at Farragut, but it was her first duty station after joining the Navy shortly after the beginning of World War II. It was also after her first brief but unhappy try at matrimony. She was not a Wave but a regular Navy officer. She was transferred to Sun Valley Navy Rehabilitation Hospital sometime at the end of 1943 or early 1944. In those days so-called fraternization with enlisted troops was not allowed for officers. Most of the male officers were already married, decreasing the pool of possible social contacts for female officers.

She met my dad some time during the first couple of months of 1944. Steve Hannagan had contacted him asking him to return to Sun Valley to publicize the Navy's work there and bring the resort back into the minds of the public again. He was to meet with the officers and the patients and take lots of pictures to show off Sun Valley. He was scheduled to meet with the commanding officer on Monday. The officers had a party at Trail Creek Cabin on Saturday night. The five nurses who were stationed there were supposed to go to Trail Creek Cabin, which served as the Officer's Club, to dance with the male officers and entertain them. Elaine was accompanying the commanding officer when he left the party, fell down the basement stairs and died that night. Very shortly afterwards Elaine received a promotion to Lieutenant JG and Daddy had to take her picture to be used in the publicity for Sun Valley. That was how they met.

CHAPTER 6

Elaine Miriam Kitchin

Rev. Sam Kitchin

Born on June 17, 1910, in Philadelphia, Elaine was the second child of Samuel Seneca and Emma Marie Wagner Kitchin. Her older sister, Dorothy Evelyn Kitchin was born December 4, 1907. Samuel's middle name came from Seneca Lake in New York. His mother, a tiny woman of about ninety pounds with a little Irish brogue, liked the name Seneca so well that she named her son that.

In her biographical notes, Elaine says she was born in the Frankfort neighborhood of Philadelphia. Frankfort seems to be spelled either Frankfort, or earlier, Frankford, but relates to the same residential area. Originally it was a small village located on Frankford Creek about six miles from Philadelphia but as Philadelphia grew it became part of Philadelphia. This residential area was

Marie Kitchin
Sam's 2nd Wife

Doris Chapin Bailey

roughly bounded by the Delaware River, Roosevelt Boulevard, Cheltenham Avenue and the original bed of the Frankford Creek. William Penn created a trail from Philadelphia through Frankford to New York City. The trail became known as "Frankford Pike" and later "Frankford Avenue".

Samuel Kitchin worked for the Post Office for nineteen years and then quit in order to go into business for himself. In her biographical notes Elaine makes the cryptic comment: "The railroad strike in 1919 was the reason Dad lost his business." I have no dates available for her father's changes of employment. Samuel and Emma Marie Wagner were married on May 18, 1904 and their first child, Dorothy Evelyn, was born on December 4, 1907. Quoting again from Elaine's notes:

> "When Dotty was just a baby she became very ill and Mother gave her a medication that she thought would help her. It had camphor in it and apparently Dotty was very allergic to camphor and went into convulsions. My father was desperate; they were doing everything to try to save this baby's life and he got down on his knees and vowed he would devote his life to Jesus Christ if Jesus would save Dotty's life. Dotty, of course, survived and Daddy kept his pledge to Jesus and started immediately studying. He went to Bible school in Philadelphia. He worked diligently to promote this great faith that he had and the gift he had received from Jesus. I was born June 17, 1910."

Elaine loved their house on Conklin Street when she was growing up. Her German grandmother lived with them for four years.

She spoke very little English and I remember Elaine speaking of her grandmother with great affection. She mentioned her grandmother's Bible, which was written in German, several times, and the fact that she loved to sing and bake. She died in 1914 of cancer of the liver.

Emma had a pet alligator which was allowed to go wherever it wanted in the house. One day the Fuller Brush man came to the front door and struck up a conversation with Emma who loved to talk. Once again, quoting from Elaine's notes:

"....he was showing her all his wares, all of the brushes, and all of a sudden Mother heard this horrible noise. Mother jumped and screamed and she said "Oh, my alligator" and she ran out. It was a very, very cold morning and she had the alligator out in the outer kitchen and she thought she would warm him up a little and turned the oven on low and put him inside and the poor thing died. When she came back she was crying to the Fuller Brush man that her alligator had died and, of course, now it has become such a joke that such a thing could ever happen, that anyone could ever love an alligator to that degree."

Dotty & Elaine Kitchen

Elaine's and Dotty's childhood was an idyllic early 20th century one. She loved their large, windowed home and the special walks with her father when he returned from work on the train early in the afternoon. She admired his steadfastness towards his God and enjoyed delivering Christian tracts to doors up and down the streets of Frankford. They had no vehicle and walked everywhere. She was fascinated by the sights and sounds she encountered; all the carts and horses each vendor used, the farrier, the milkman, and her Uncle Charles, who was a delivery man who frequently picked her up at school on Mondays and brought her home for lunch and delivered her back to school with his beautiful horse and wagon. (Was this Uncle Charles her father's brother or her mother's?) Philadelphia's well known brick and cobblestone streets were hard on the horses and hard on those who were riding in the wagon, but she loved it all. There was the man who sold "fresh pretzels" which were so tasty with mustard and pickles and the ice cream man with several kinds of ice cream, including one he called "micka" which she spent considerable time wondering what it was. Eventually he explained that when he started running low on his various kinds of ice cream, he would put them all together in one container and called the mixture "micka."

Dotty spent most of her spare time reading, but Elaine loved to play outside and watch the people, running and playing games. One of the wooden toys she remembered you could sit on and pull the handle back and forth and scoot around on it. She could go all the way around the block, which was a great deal of fun.

Sam was an inveterate inventor. He made Emma a vacuum cleaner, which he hooked up to a bicycle in the basement. He would pedal the bicycle furiously while his wife was cleaning the rugs and floors around the house. However, Emma loved to talk and occasionally would forget Samuel pumping away on the bicycle so she could vacuum. She would begin a conversation with Mrs. Simmons, the next door neighbor, and be thoroughly enjoying it when she would hear Sam call to her saying, "Emma, we're working, remember, don't talk, we've got to get this done."

Life was very busy for Sam in these years. He worked, went to school and spent a great deal of time at the Galilee Mission in downtown Philadelphia. He taught his daughters how to pray daily and read their Bible. He never forgot he had to make a living and fulfill his promise to devote his life to Jesus. Elaine told me one time that her father wanted very much to become a minister but Emma was adamantly opposed to being "the preacher's wife" so he continued as he always had done. I have tried to determine exactly what occupation he had over the years, both by reading her notes and by remembering conversations. I have not been successful. I was told at one time he was a civil engineer. Then I read that he worked for the post office for almost twenty years and then started a business which failed. He took the train daily about 4 a.m. to work and returned in mid-afternoon at which time he spent time with his daughters, delivered Christian tracts and brought a good number of people home to eat. These included well-known successful people as well as those who were down and out and needed charity. Elaine remembers a visit from Helen Keller.

Emma enjoyed taking all the neighborhood children, as well as Dotty and Elaine, on picnics. They would go all the way from Frankford to Fairmount Park to the zoo, a tremendous ride on the streetcar, with several changes. Sometimes they would go see the Liberty Bell or to Betsy Ross's house or to one of the many other historic houses in that small area of Philadelphia where the history of our country is so interwoven. The Galilee Mission, where Sam helped out three nights a week, was also in this area.

One particular person remained in Elaine's memory for her lifetime was a young drug addict who Sam especially felt had a lot of potential, Charles Monroe. Sam helped him get off drugs and go to seminary and become a minister in the Episcopal Church. Some years later, his wife died and Charles fell in love with his secretary, who was married. Her husband came looking for her at one time and Charles killed the husband and went to jail. Elaine never heard what happened to him after that point. Charles' mother lived with Sam and Emma for a long time.

Sam decided to quit his job at the post office. Emma was extremely opposed to this move but Sam had an idea to make some kind of waste cloth and found a friend who would finance the operation. Emma spent a lot of time trying to help Sam make a success of this venture, but the railway strike occurred about the time Elaine turned nine, and their success withered. Sam was offered a job in Chicago and he took it and left Philadelphia. This was a very difficult and traumatic time for the family. They were separated for three years. The house in Philadelphia was sold and they were to move to Chicago. Emma decided they would make it a surprise for Sam and so didn't tell him they were coming. When they arrived in Chicago they were unable to contact Sam and had to find a hotel to stay in. He was working for the Gideon's and was out preaching when they arrived. Sam was horrified when he found out late that night they were there in Chicago because he didn't want them to live in Chicago. So the next day he sent them to Wheaton because it was supposed to be such a good Christian community and he was sure their lives would be much better if they were living there.

They found lodgings in the Wheaton Hotel the following day but discovered the place was overrun with bedbugs. They sat in straight back chairs all night. Emma went out and bought two mattresses, they found a house to rent and used these mattresses while their household belongings were coming from Philadelphia. Sometime shortly after this move Elaine learned to drive an automobile. Sam purchased a brand new Overland car, which included driving lessons for someone. He decided that someone would be Elaine. Dotty had no desire to drive and Sam would not consider his wife driving, so Elaine became the family chauffeur. She was about 12 or 13. For the rest of her life, she loved driving. She also acquired a love of driving fast. In her later years, she got many speeding tickets and was the butt of many family jokes about her fast driving. Fortunately she was not in any serious auto accidents, nor the cause of any. She drove her dad to the train station to catch the train into Chicago for his work and she drove Dotty to school.

Dotty went to Wheaton Academy for one year and then transferred to the local college. Elaine went to Wheaton for two unhappy years before her parents allowed her to go to the local public high school. According to Elaine many things were happening to cause her parents to become disenchanted with Wheaton Academy. The President of the Academy required marriage of students caught kissing or driving in an automobile together. He believed it was impossible for a girl and boy together to do either of these things without becoming sexually involved.

At church one evening he accused a young man of stealing money. This young man was living in the President's home and had been sent by the President's wife to buy groceries at the local store. These were charged to the President's account. He frequently was sent on errands such as this. On occasion, the young man would return a small item to the store, requesting a refund which he apparently then spent. Emma was enraged over this public accusal. The boy had been sent directly to the President and his wife with $4,000, a large sum of money in the 1920's, to attend Wheaton and to pay all his living costs but was never given any spending money at all. He was the grandson of a well-known missionary to China. In addition, he had been required to do a lot of work around the President's home, such as taking care of the furnace and mowing the law, as well as shopping and running errands. Doing these odd jobs did seem appropriate, however, and no protest was given for that. However Emma strongly objected to the charge of stealing, so she jumped up in church the evening he was accused and, according to Elaine's account, Emma aid, "President Blanchard, I want all of those slips. I will pay for all of those slips. I want that boy. He will live in my home." With that, she went right up to the altar....got her checkbook out and wrote a check to President Blanchard for the amount he claimed the boy had stolen. Alfred came to live with us and he was a precious.....person."

Elaine begged her parents to let her leave Wheaton and go to the local high school because a young black girl developed a crush on her. She kept hanging around Elaine, kissing her and hugging her, sitting on their doorstep waiting for Elaine to come home and constantly trying to be close to her. She was told she should try to "love" this girl but Elaine was unable to do that and continued begging her parents to allow her to leave Wheaton Academy. She had constantly received grades between 85 and 95, which was certainly acceptable, but when Emma went to Wheaton to tell them Elaine was going to go to a different school, she was told that would probably be difficult because Elaine was failing English. Since English was Elaine's best subject, Emma immediately challenged the Wheaton representative, saying that she had in her possession Elaine's report cards showing decent grades. The President responded by opening a drawer and presenting Emma with a list of four themes that he required Elaine to write in order to get a passing grade in English. Emma promptly went home and distributed the four subjects: one to Sam, one to Dotty, one to Elaine and one for herself. Elaine withdrew from Wheaton. Dotty had already enrolled in Northern Illinois State Normal School in DeKalb to be a teacher. This is where she met Tom Altenderfer. They were married June 29, 1929.

An unsavory experience happened to Elaine one morning when she drove her dad to the train station for his daily trip to Chicago. She merrily waved to the policeman who was standing at the train station every morning and he stopped her for some conversation, saying, "What a beautiful car! I have never driven a car like that. Would you mind if I drove it around the block?" Elaine handed him the keys. He asked her to drive around the block with him and for some reason, she climbed into the car.

He drove out in the country and according to her notes, she spent seven hours talking to him about God and being a child of God and fighting him off. She concludes by saying "I guess nothing happened to me and I was able to talk continuously to this man and convince him that I was a child of God and that he could not do this to me." When she got home her father's sister, her Aunt Ida, who was visiting from Philadelphia, and her mother were frantic with worry. Aunt Ida told her she should never be without a hat pin. She responded by wondering what she would do with a hat pin!

The summer of 1927 Elaine graduated from high school. She and Dotty had decided to go to Colorado Springs to go to college. They lived in a house their father rented for them and got jobs at the local hotel. Elaine became a waitress in the dining room and Dotty became a manicurist in their salon. They had a happy summer but Sam and Emma were in a terrible auto accident when some Al Capone gangsters ran a stop sign and hit them. Dotty and Elaine dropped everything and went directly back to take care of their parents. By the time they got home their parents were well on the way to recovery and Elaine found herself at loose ends. She wanted to go to nurse's training, but had a hard time getting any nursing school to accept her because she not only was young but definitely looked young. She was finally accepted at West Suburban Hospital in Oak Park, Illinois. The superintendent there kept telling her to "try to make yourself look older." The nursing program was three years long, so she expected to graduate in 1932. I'm not sure how much financial help she might have had from her father. The stock market crashed in October of 1929 and the time lines are fuzzy in Elaine's narrative. Sam did lose money in the crash, as he had invested, although I don't know how heavily.

Elaine found herself falling in love with a young man named John "Jack" Cardwell. He had a fairly large family and it can be deduced from Elaine's notes that she was fond of Jack's sisters and nieces. In August 1931 she and Jack "ran away and got married." In that day and age she would have immediately been expelled from her nursing school if they had known she had married. Sam and Emma were living in St. Louis during this time and Elaine seldom saw them. Jack, who was a successful insurance adjuster, suddenly decided to study to become an attorney. Elaine took some postgraduate work at Chicago State Hospital for seven months which, according to Elaine, caused Jack to become upset because she had more education than he did. He began studying at the John Marshall Law School in Chicago. They must have been having trouble making ends meet because Elaine received no pay when she was going to nursing school except for having her uniforms cleaned and being able to get her meals at the hospital. However, she was with Jack for seven years and only one of those years was she taking her nursing training.

Elaine talks about Jack going to school at night and working all day alluding to the strains of making a living. She also mentions that he started doing odd things, which included slamming the car door on her elbow. They had bought a beautiful home in Villa Park. Elaine was thrilled about the home but as they were moving out of their apartment, Jack got angry with her and tried to choke her. Elaine left him and went to Philadelphia immediately to help her mother take care of her aunt, who was quite ill. Jack came to Philadelphia and begged Elaine to come back to him, which she did. However, Jack soon took up playing with a gun in the house and making comments about using it. She felt he was planning to use it on her. She went to a friend who was a psychiatrist at Chicago State Hospital and arranged for this friend to come for dinner. The psychiatrist made friends with Jack and talked Jack into spending a considerable amount of time with him over the next few months. The friend finally contacted Elaine and told her she definitely needed to divorce Jack. He felt that Jack somewhere in his mind would try to kill Elaine. Elaine left Jack and went to work in an emergency ward at Cook County Hospital. She loved the work but couldn't get rid of Jack, who continued to hound her, frequently being there when she got off work, getting into her room and trashing it and doing other bizarre things. They were officially divorced on December 27, 1938.

Emma went to visit the New York World's Fair which opened April 30, 1939, and was open for two seasons between April and October each year. It was a huge financial failure and ended a year before the United States entered World War II. While Emma was vacationing at the World's Fair she caught meningitis. Elaine dropped everything and went directly to her mother, but there was nothing anyone could do to fight this disease and her mother died. Elaine was devastated.

A few weeks later she went to Sam with an idea she was sure he would be as excited about as she was. She had gotten accepted into medical school to become a doctor and had everything paid for except for room and board. She suggested to her dad that she would keep house for him and do the cooking in exchange for room and board so that she could become a doctor. Sam sat down very slowly and sadly and took Elaine's hands in his and said, "I am very sorry

Elaine but I am marrying Marie (his secretary of twenty plus years) and that will not be possible." With Sam's marriage to Marie he was able to accomplish his longtime desire to become a minister. He had finished seminary so he completed the process and became ordained and found a church. He got his PhD at age 86 and had a very fulfilling and happy new career.

Marie and Sam made one cross country trip to visit us in Idaho. They enjoyed the travel and seeing our large country very much. Marie made one comment which always makes me smile when I hear it. "The West is really something! You can drive all day and be in the same state!" I liked Sam Kitchin and his wife, Marie, even though I only was privileged to visit with Grandpa Kitchin the one time. He never talked down to me and we had some wonderful conversations about careers and life and many things. I was always very grateful to have met him. Marie continued visiting every few years until her death in the 1990's. I don't know how old Marie was, but she was apparently not much older than Elaine.

When war was declared December 8, 1941, after the Japanese had bombed Pearl Harbor on the 7th, Elaine went down to sign up for Unit 13 from Presbyterian Hospital because they had gained so much fame in World War I. However, she had injured her back on a trip to visit relatives with Dotty, and the Army would not take her. She worked privately as a nurse for a wealthy lady named Mary Ross until the Navy called her. She was sent to Great Lakes and from there to Farragut in Northern Idaho. Her original orders were for her to leave Farragut for Attu in Alaska but the Navy discovered her experience in psychiatric nursing and at the last minute sent her to Sun Valley. Sun Valley never hid Elaine from Jack. He came to Sun Valley and she had quite a time getting rid of him, but that was finally the last time she saw him.

Ellis 'Chape' & Elaine Chapin

CHAPTER 7

The First Years of My Second Life

The wedding of my dad and Elaine enabled a shopping trip for me, as I wanted to buy a wedding gift for them. It took me more than an hour but I finally found a bathroom set in pretty black and red chenille that I liked and that fit the amount of money I had available for this gift. I was very gratified that it was used for many years.

The house we lived in that year of 1944-45 was about three miles about three miles outside of Ketchum near the Wood River and across the road from Jay and Helen Fassett's beautiful home, which they named River's Edge Ranch. Jay and Helen were Elaine's friends and were connected to New York City's Broadway theater scene. I believe Helen was an actress and Jay was involved in production. They were Daddy and Elaine's matron of honor and best man at their wedding.

Ours was a small house but very comfortable. It was about half a mile from a service station which was run by a couple with a daughter my age. Marjorie McHan and I became close friends and had many good times together during the months we lived there. Apparently my dad didn't tell Elaine that his mother divided her time between Uncle Phil's and his house, because she was quite upset when she found out they had to go to Blackfoot to collect Daddy's mother. The little house only had two bedrooms, which Elaine had fixed up to be a bedroom for me and one for them. The upstairs was simply an attic with no floor.

Daddy moved their bed into the attic area but made no move to put a floor down until Elaine simply could not contain her unhappiness, telling him that she couldn't live that way and would have to leave if he didn't arrange a better bedroom for her. He immediately put a floor down in the attic area and they wallpapered. It had windows in both ends which let light in, so, all in all, it was a pleasant little room. I was given the upstairs attic room and Daddy and Elaine gave my room to Grandma Chapin and took their own original bedroom back for themselves. I loved that attic bedroom and remember gazing out at night at the stars and looking at the clouds in the shape of horses and dragons and covered wagons.

Grandma Chapin lived with us for several months. One time she fell down the basement stairs, got up and said, "Damn, I opened the wrong door." Although I didn't ever know her as well as Grandma Andersen, I knew she had a sense of humor. By the time I entered 6th grade she had decided she wanted to live in the Odd Fellows and Rebekkah's Home for the elderly in Caldwell. She loved that home and would come to visit us for two or three days and then say, "Ellis, I'm ready to go home now." They had people she enjoyed and a piano which she could play at any time. She was comfortable and happy and Daddy was close enough to go see her often.

Elaine learned how to cook on a wood stove in our little house because that was the only stove available. It took her a while, but she seemed to enjoy it. We had a big snowstorm that year that closed the roads and schools and turned the electricity off for many hours. Margie and I had an absolutely wonderful time taking hot coffee and soup in thermoses to the two or three neighbors.

We felt very heroic!

The railroad tracks ran not more than a quarter of a mile behind our house to Ketchum. This conveyance was the primary transport for the sheep in the fall. It was an old fashioned fire-stoked steam engine. One time it started a fire in the sagebrush between the tracks and our house as well as Margie's house toward Ketchum. I was home by myself and got a little excited, but within just a short time there were numerous people out in the sagebrush fighting the fire. It came within fifteen or twenty feet of our house, but was stopped. It didn't get close to McHan's service station at all. It was an adventure though to an eleven-year-old.

Elaine found 52 acres of beautiful desert valley that she fell in love with. It was called the Owl Rock land and she started going down to Gannett to the elderly owner's home to ask about buying this property. He was a devout Mormon and before he would discuss the property he insisted that she read several books about his religion. After she had been visiting him for several months she used what she had left in her savings and borrowed some money from Olga Beautmiller, the Director of Nurses at Sun Valley, talked Daddy into buying it and paid $1,400 for it. I went up to see it one time and it truly was breathtaking property which undoubtedly would increase in value as Sun Valley prospered and grew.

In the middle of the summer we started noticing a white spot on the mountains across the Wood River from us. We watched it for several days until Daddy couldn't stand it any longer and took off early one morning with his camera to climb up there to determine what it was. It was late in the day before he got back and explained that it was a huge mushroom of some sort. When he developed the pictures everyone was very interested to see this huge fungus amidst all the sagebrush on the hillside near the top of the mountain. I loved to play in the hills behind our house, either with Margie or by myself. It was mostly sagebrush and rocky outcroppings with a tiny creek seeping down and across an open area with aspens shading the creek. That creek usually had delicious watercress, which I loved to gather and take home for meals. It always made me think of Galena summit, where Alturas and Red Fish Lake were located and where we went for camping trips and fishing in the summers. I especially enjoyed Red Fish Lake because on the other side of the lake you could climb up to where the "lily pond" was located. To get there we usually took one of the little row boats that were available and Daddy rowed us across. It was beautiful up there and I always loved the watercress we found up there too. One time a camera was accidentally left at the lily pond and Daddy had to row back across the lake and climb up to the pond to retrieve it. When I was a young girl, there was always snow still up on the mountain tops where Galena Summit perched above Sun Valley to the north. Daddy took a lot of pictures one time for a publicity blitz about making ice cream with the snow at Galena Summit on the

4th of July. A friend of mine had come with us to Galena Summit to pose with me for the pictures Daddy made. I remember it being quite a lot of fun. A lot of picturesque gorgeous scenery was ruined when the road was improved and widened to a modern four lane road, which is much safer now than it was then, but less scenic. Stanley and the Salmon River country of central Idaho were true wilderness and scenic panoramas.

The same is true for the Wood River valley where I played as a girl. I frequently would see coyotes and rabbits and was warned to watch for rattlesnakes, which I never saw but I suspect were there if I'd been looking a bit more carefully. I climbed rocks and found snug little hiding places all day long, thoroughly enjoying the long hot summer days. When I had a playmate we played daredevil, running across the railroad bridge over the Wood River and other types of "shoot 'em up" games. Fortunately the train only traversed the tracks once a day or it may have been more dangerous than it was. Sadly, the idyllic life was coming to an end.

I had started 6th grade in our small eight grade school and Daddy had gone off on a hunting trip with some celebrities. According to Elaine's notes she was staying with the Fassetts because she had an infection needing penicillin shots. I'm not sure what my situation was. In any event, Daddy and his hunting group got caught in a huge blizzard and the plane which was scheduled to go pick them up couldn't fly. Bing Crosby was also scheduled to arrive in Sun Valley to entertain and Daddy was expected to be there to take pictures. According to her notes, Elaine said Crosby came out to the Fassett's and begged her to come into Sun Valley to the arranged party but she felt so badly that Daddy wasn't there that she declined the invitation. Steve Hannagan was so upset that he sent word that Daddy was no longer needed at Sun Valley. Elaine and Daddy were stunned and at a loss as to what to do. Elaine had been helping with the administrative end of the photography that Daddy had been doing and so she was also out of work.

CHAPTER 8

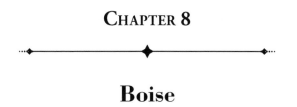

Boise

The Statesman newspaper in Boise had decided to challenge the Twin Falls paper for circulation in Twin Falls and they sent Daddy to Twin to work for them. That was a very confusing time for me because I didn't understand what was happening. I had started 6th grade in Ketchum, was transferred to Twin Falls, where I attended a few weeks and then was sent to St. Teresa's Academy, a Catholic boarding school in Boise for the rest of 6th grade. I don't really remember Twin Falls at all, except for the physical education class. I never liked any of the gym classes I had to take in school and for some reason those are the classes that stayed in my mind the most. We weren't in Twin Falls very long when the Statesman dropped their Twin Falls venture and Daddy transferred to Boise, working as a newspaper photographer. We lived in Boise from late 1945 to the summer of 1951. Elaine's notes indicate that other than the short time short time in Twin Falls, Daddy was out of work for over a year. I cannot confirm nor deny that because I do not remember. Elaine got work almost immediately at the Rapid Treatment Center which treated sexually transmitted diseases with which our servicemen were coming home. Elaine worked there and at St. Luke's Hospital during the time we lived in Boise.

When we first moved to Boise we lived in a downtown hotel. Daddy and Elaine didn't want me in the hotel by myself so they put me in St. Teresa's. St. Teresa's was very difficult for me. I had never been in a large city school and had no knowledge of Catholicism. The first thing that happened was the ridicule I endured from the nuns over the clothes I wore. I always wore long brown cotton stockings in the wintertime to keep my legs warm. Girls never wore pants to school in those days and wearing a dress in the cold Blackfoot or Sun Valley winter was very uncomfortable. Since I needed to take care of my shoes and not get them wet because shoes cost a lot of money and couldn't be replaced easily, I usually wore ski boots to school and then changed. For some reason, the nuns felt the long stockings and the ski boots were quite amusing and I was soon begging my parents for regular shoes with anklets to wear to school.

I had also learned to do arithmetic by counting on my fingers. I was very fast at it and had never been caught up to this time. However, at St. Teresa's the sharp-eyed nuns quickly realized what I was doing and I was relegated to another room for arithmetic time until I had learned addition and subtraction without using my fingers. Actually I was quite pleased about the arithmetic dilemma and was glad to be able to add and subtract so quickly. Learning the 9's from Esther Skoog came in very handy and I use that method to this day. The Mother Superior made a habit of visiting all the rooms at least once a week. When she arrived in a classroom everyone stood up in respect. She then wrote a long series of numbers on the chalkboard and called a student forward. That student had to add the numbers up out loud. If there was too long a pause in the addition, the student was scolded and another student called to the board. I have a competitive streak in me and it didn't take very long before I could add and subtract as fast as anyone. Although I never was really happy at St. Teresa's I was always glad about learning the math.

I had always wanted a bike and finally received one when I was a student at St. Teresa's. That was a wonderful gift and although the bike was not a new one it was very presentable and I loved it. I rode it regularly until I learned to drive at age sixteen. A postscript to this information is that in Idaho at that time, a person could receive a learner's driving permit at age fourteen. However, my parents felt fourteen was way too young to drive and didn't allow me to drive until I was sixteen. My dad bartered driving lessons for me in return for advertising pictures for the firm who sold driving lessons. Thus I learned how to drive from taking a several week course which included actual driving in a specially outfitted car.

My parents found a motel room equipped with a small kitchen in the Green Gables Motel on the outskirts of Boise, and then later a small apartment in an old "changed-from-motel-to-apartment" building and were able to bring me back to live with them instead of boarding at St. Teresa's. Apparently neither were in a "nice" part of Boise, but there were lots of other kids my age living nearby and I enjoyed it with all that unaccustomed company. Grandma Chapin stayed with us a few weeks, sleeping in the living room, when we lived in the motel changed to apartment. I frequently walked and talked in my sleep and it was there that I went in and woke Grandma up one night and asked her to please bait my hook. She said, "ok it's baited" and I went back to bed. That made a good story which was often told in family circles. One of my favorite activities was playing baseball in the empty lot next door. That sounds very suspicious after my comment that I didn't like physical education. However, playing baseball with the neighborhood kids in an empty lot with no adults to insist on certain rules, carries a huge amount of excitement to kids who can discuss a change in rules and initiate it without anyone objecting. What a lot of fun!

Daddy was finally working at the Statesman newspaper and he and Elaine found a home being built on 31st Street which they were qualified to use a veteran's loan to purchase due to Elaine's years in the Navy. What a wonderful day it was when we moved into that house. There were two bedrooms downstairs and a bedroom upstairs similar to my bedroom in the Ketchum house. We had a huge yard, which my parents fenced in. It was a wonderful house to me. We were two blocks from State Street where I could catch the bus to school. We lived in that house for five years and it was a place I really enjoyed.

I started school at Boise Junior High School for 7th, 8th and 9th and then on to Boise High School for 10th and 11th. I loved school and always got very good grades. I remember that 7th grade was the first time students were allowed to have an elective. That was very exciting and I spent a long time going over the list of electives, since I could only choose one. I ended up choosing drama and loved it so much that I continued through all the years of schooling after that. In junior high school the drama teacher was Clara McGrath and in high school it was Ludwig Gerner. I remember those teachers to this day and appreciate how much influence they had on me to do well and to live life fully. Although I did enjoy acting, especially since I was attracted to the lime light, I ended up liking directing and gathering props the most.

As usual, I loved school and thrived in the large student body and large building. I became active in Girl Scouts and our Presbyterian church youth group as well as the various school activities which included drama classes. The two plays a year that were staged gave me a chance to learn and show off. There was a competition yearly called a "declamation contest" that I especially enjoyed. My favorite event was the dramatic reading which was different from the way competitions are handled in Southeast Alaska, where I live now. The pieces were supposed to be at least ten minutes long and no more than twenty minutes and had to be memorized. Then you acted them out. I not only enjoyed doing my own piece but I enjoyed watching all the others. In the summer I started going to Girl Scout Camp and church camp at Payette Lake near McCall. Then most of the rest of the summer I spent in Blackfoot with my grandparents.

I was just finished with 7th grade when my first sister, Vicki Elaine, was born June 24, 1947. I was in Blackfoot and didn't learn about my new sister for a considerable time. It was a terrible delivery for Elaine. She was in labor 72 hours before they decided to do a Caesarian section. They used high forceps on her for hours before they decided to do the section. Elaine was beside herself. According to her notes, "They had promised me....... they would never use forceps on my baby...... they kept giving me things that would knock me out so I couldn't complain about anything. This was all night long they were trying to do this. Finally at 8:30 in the morning the baby's heart beats were so bad, my condition was very bad. They decided to do a C section. This is something that really and truly should never be done, after all this fussing around with forceps and everything....... Finally Vicki was born on that morning and my bladder was damaged. They forgot to catheterize me....... I was unconscious for four days and four nights." Aunt Dotty had come out from Chicago on June 1st and was still there when Vicki was born on the 24th. Elaine was so ill that even though they discharged her she couldn't take care of Vicki, so Dotty took Vicki and went home to Chicago. Elaine was in such terrible pain that she was finally put back in the hospital. She couldn't use her left leg at all and the pain was excruciating. Dr. Ralph Jones had taken over Elaine's care since she didn't want to see the former doctor ever again. Dr. Jones had her leg put in traction, which relieved a lot of the pain and she was finally able to get away from the powerful pain medications she was on and after a considerable amount of time she was able to come home again.

Elaine, Vicki & Gayle

Late in the fall Elaine was able to go back to Chicago to get Vicki. Aunt Dotty had Vicki for so long that she wanted to keep her. Elaine, of course, was horrified by the idea and instantly refused to even discuss the idea. Elaine and Vicki finally got home sometime after school had started that year.

Sometime in 1948, Daddy was in Alaska with Frank Morrison of Morrison, Knudson Corporation to photograph the construction on the Alcan Highway and to train the photographer that Knudson had hired. He was gone for several weeks training this photographer how to take pictures of the road building along with other construction being done by the company in Alaska. He got home some time in September or October. Elaine was thrilled because the doctor had told her she could now try for a second child.

The doctors did the Caesarian section for Gayle Yvonne on May 11, 1949. They took her a month early because they wanted to avoid any problems that might occur because of the bad delivery of Vicki. She weighed 4 lbs. 14-1/2 oz. and was soon up to 5 lbs., which was the required weight before she could go home. Aunt Mary was having a baby at exactly the same time but Grandma Andersen decided that Mary had several other relatives willing and able to go help her, so Grandma came to Boise to take care of Elaine and the new baby, as well as Vicki. Grandma stayed a couple of weeks to help out. She was a very good sport and made every effort to do everything the way Elaine wanted it done, which Aunt Dot mentioned to me one time that Grandma thought was way more than anybody should do. I did the ironing for the little girls but was never allowed to babysit or take care of them.

I "graduated" from junior high school that May and was so thrilled because Grandma came to my graduation ceremony. Daddy or Elaine never came to any of my school activities, so this was a very exciting thing to happen. Usually my two camps happened consecutively after school was out and then I went to Blackfoot for the rest of the summer. I had never gotten to see Vicki until after she came home from Chicago so I was looking forward to being with my two little sisters that summer. However, the summer proceeded as it usually did and I was sent off on the train to Blackfoot after my camps were finished. I was a little put off, but Blackfoot was always fun so it was easy to accept being there.

The next two years were busy and exciting, as high school years are supposed to be. Elaine went back to work and hired the grandmother of one of my girlfriends to babysit. We called her "Steena", I don't remember what her real name was. She was a lovely lady and I liked her a lot.

I filled my time with school activities. I was admitted to the National Honor Society, Thespians and Spanish club as well as continuing Girl Scouts and youth activities at the Presbyterian Church. My drama classes also took a lot of after school time when we were working on a play. Since we lived on the city bus line there was never a problem with transportation because the bus ran every half hour and I could easily get home from the school or church at any time. As happens in high school, I had a group of ten to fifteen kids with whom I had a friendly relationship. I loved to give parties and Elaine was good about allowing that once a year and it was always exciting to have a scavenger hunt or plan other kinds of activities that teens enjoyed.

Our church youth group decided we wanted to help a Displaced Person. These were people who had been "displaced" by World War II. Their homes were now in countries where they couldn't return. There were thousands of these people in the late 40's that were being relocated around the world. We did, in fact, bring a family to Boise to live. There was a huge amount of paperwork.

We had to promise a job, a place to live and support, I believe, for three years. A Hungarian family of four arrived and, we discovered, they did not speak English. We finally found someone who spoke German and they also spoke German, so communication was established. Eventually we found someone who spoke Hungarian. The job we had been promised at the dairy had disappeared by the time the family arrived in Boise, but we were able to find a job at the optometrist making lenses. The displaced man had been some sort of professional man before the war. I am awed today by the students, all of whom were members of our Presbyterian youth group, and the adults who supported those students. Those adults undoubtedly had a lot more to do with the project's success than they allowed us as teenagers to realize. The whole youth group was at the train station when they arrived and it was very exciting. My drama teacher, Mr. Gerner, was one of those who spoke other languages and tried to bring about communication using Czech and Yugoslavian but they didn't speak either language. It was Mr. Gerner who established that they spoke German and we needed to find someone who could speak that language. That was soon accomplished and our Hungarian family began their new life in Boise.

The years we spent in Boise were undoubtedly the happiest of my new life. Elaine and I had a rocky relationship but it smoothed out somewhat and I found my niche that gave me sufficient freedom to follow my dreams. I loved school, the church youth group, Girl Scouts, the various people who were school mates and allowed me into their group, the parties that I gave and Elaine supported, and the drama classes including the plays with which I was able to help.

I did not have any close friends although I did not realize it at the time. Several things contributed to this. Although I had two baby sisters I was not allowed to babysit and my connection to them was somewhat occasional. I did the ironing on a weekly basis for them and since Elaine always had them wearing darling little dresses, they wore one in the morning and a different one each afternoon, which caused a considerably large set of clothes to be ironed. My "only child" status had not prepared me to learn how to deal with young children and I frequently found myself being scolded for the things I did do for them. It was much easier to fill my life with my own activities and continue in a teenager's self-absorbed mode than to try to figure out on my own the way one should act with small children. So I continued in my own little world, getting good grades and being as busy as possible.

The summer between my junior and senior years was a watershed year as my life changed drastically once again and I began what I call my third life.

Chapter 9

My Third Life

The summer of 1951 started out with a very exciting two week drama course for high school students going into their senior year that was being given at the University of Idaho in Moscow. I had been picked for Girls State and had to make the choice between the course in Moscow and that. It had seemed an easy choice to me, although it took me two days to decide. Mr. Gerner had decided that the following year he was going to pick two or three drama students and place them in the beginning classrooms to help him. I was one who was chosen and I was very excited about the idea and looking forward to the experience. This definitely influenced my decision to go to Moscow.

The course was really a good one and I enjoyed it and learned a lot. I also had my first boyfriend in Moscow. We spent almost all our evenings together and had a marvelous time. I was sure I was in love and wrote to him every day after I came home. However, he never wrote back and he quickly became history. I don't even remember his name now.

When I got home from the Moscow experience I went for my summer visit to Blackfoot and acquired my second boyfriend, Don Carpenter. My grandparents, not surprisingly, checked this young man's bona fides and determined that his family connections were good, so they gave their blessing to our relationship. We spent hours talking to one another, going to movies and picnics and not paying attention to anyone else. He gave me his high school class ring and we continued our absentee attachment for the next two years. He was a good kind of person for me to have for my first long term interest. He was from a good family as far as my grandparents were concerned. He was courteous and moral, which was certainly good for me, being very uneducated in sexual matters. This was also good because of my tremendous need for acceptance and approval. I was very lucky that I was not taken advantage of at this period of my life. Don and I corresponded two or three times a month. He joined the navy very soon after we graduated from high school the following school year.

In addition to my first experience with a male-female relationship that summer, a telephone call totally upended my plans and expectations for my senior year in high school. Just a few days before I was scheduled to go back to Boise for school that fall Elaine phoned Blackfoot to say that they had bought a new business and had moved from Boise to Nampa, Idaho. The move was already completed. Everything, including a new home, was already occupied by the family. The business was being operated by Daddy and Elaine. It consisted of a photographic equipment store including cameras and accessories, along with a studio which had contracts to do the annual pictures for Northwest Nazarene College and Nampa High School. I was devastated because all the plans I had made for my senior year were gone. I had never easily made new friends and the normal attitude of high school students about newcomers seemed to take direct aim at me. I had spent five years in the Boise school system and knew the buildings, the students, the teachers and the climate of the system. It was the longest I had ever spent in one town's school system. I had first, second and half of third grade in Ketchum, the rest of third and fourth in Blackfoot, fifth in Ketchum again, sixth at St. Teresa's in Boise and then from seventh through eleventh in the public school system in Boise. I had always been active in various school activities and had a group of kids with whom I associated and who I considered friends.

Nampa High School was a very different place. They had various activities supporting school varsity sports. These groups required that you had to have participated in them during the two previous years to be able to join them in the senior year. I was able to become active in their drama classes and enjoyed them and the teacher, Mr. Terwilliger. The school also required a year of economics to graduate, which I hadn't taken. Students usually took this class in their junior year, but since it was needed for graduation I needed to take it my senior year. I spent the year limping along scholastically and attending very few extracurricular activities other than drama. I had as friends almost exclusively students who were new to the high school, as I was. Amazingly when I graduated I still had an overall high school grade average which was the tenth highest out of the three hundred fifty seniors graduating. I can still distinctly remember standing very alone on the steps of the school after the graduation ceremony, looking around at everyone dashing off to all the individual parties and celebrations being held, and wondering "Now what?" The lost feeling I had at that moment was unlike anything I'd ever experienced either before or since.

In looking back after the intervening sixty years, I realize that most, if not all, of the acting out and problems and changes in my behavior which occurred during that year were probably due to the upset I was feeling over the move. It took me many years to realize what a good thing the move was for my dad and Elaine. Daddy was so happy working sixteen to eighteen hours a day, seven days a week to keep up. They had kept on a young man who had been working there for several years, Jerry Cornelius, who had a lot of the information needed on the logistics of running a busy photo shop. Jerry was invaluable in selling the camera equipment, which Daddy had never done, and in arranging and keeping track of the huge multiple photo orders from the schools. Elaine knew nothing about photography and had not had any interest in it, but when they embarked on this new adventure, she packed all her nurse's uniforms and other medical paraphernalia into a trunk and made the conscious decision to learn everything possible about photography so she could become one of the best there was. I remember her telling me that here was her life as a nurse (in the trunk) but she was giving it up to have a successful photography business. As the years went by she did become an expert portraiture photographer while Daddy continued doing the commercial work, especially the rodeo pictures of the Snake River Stampede and construction projects for Morrison, Knudson and Idaho Power Company, among others.

During the rodeo, Daddy worked long into every night so that day's pictures would be developed, printed and ready for the rodeo contestants and others to buy. He won the "Rodeo Picture of the Year" on more than one occasion and became well known for his magnificent action photos. I don't know what organization presented this award. There are many rodeo organizations and the way rodeos are given today are completely different in many ways from the way they were in the 40's and 50's. In my teen years the so-called top three rodeos were the Calgary Stampede (Alberta, Canada), the Pendleton, Oregon, Roundup and the Cheyenne, Wyoming, rodeo. Daddy was the official photographer for the Snake River Stampede held annually in Nampa, Idaho.

One year Daddy was gored in the knee by an angry bull who did not want to be ridden and was saved by the rodeo clowns. The clowns were always the heroes of the entire spectacle because they were there primarily to attract the animals away from a downed person so that person could be gotten quickly from the ring and given whatever medical attention he needed. Rodeo can be an exciting thing to watch and it can be very dangerous. Injuries and even deaths do occur. When Elaine got to the hospital to see Daddy, he greeted her in his usual way, "Did you get a picture?" She hadn't.

The Professional Photographers of Idaho was started by Daddy and Elaine. They made the organization into a well run and successful group for photographers around the state. Meetings were frequently held in their shop and they began to be asked to both show their photos and to judge in various photo shows around the country. They also gave classes and seminars on photographic subjects both in the United States and in other countries.

Selling photographic equipment was something neither Daddy nor Elaine liked doing so within a very short time they sold that part of the business and bought a house in which they could live and, with very little remodeling, turn into a studio. They kept the studio open for business until the early 80's. It gave them a great deal of self-satisfaction and afforded them a decent living.

Daddy decided to retire when he turned 65 in the late 60's which disappointed Elaine because they were at the top of their success and she was enjoying the work. I suspect a good part of the decision may have been Daddy's lack of enthusiasm for portraiture and weariness of the physical hard work of commercial photography. His knee injury caused by the bull continued to haunt him until he finally agreed to have total knee replacement. This surgery was in its infancy at the time, and, with the use of stainless steel instead of the synthetic composites used later, was not as comfortable. To do the commercial photography the way he wanted it done frequently required him to climb with a large and heavy amount of equipment for considerable distances in steep, rough terrain. Elaine continued to do portraiture and kept the studio open until her eyesight became so poor that she was not satisfied with the quality of the pictures she made. She had contracted a terrible case of shingles, which ran across her head and down into her eyes, causing lesions which affected her sight. With her realization that Daddy was not going to be able to continue to assist her and when even a cornea transplant did not improve her sight sufficiently, she realized she would need to retire.

CHAPTER 10

My Third Life Continues

However, 1951 was the beginning of Ellis and Elaine Chapin's adventure in having their own business and becoming well known for their skills and artistic abilities. I survived my difficult senior year of high school and then turned my attentions to attending college.

My first priority after graduating from high school was to find a job so that I could help pay for college. A local lady doctor with two four and five year old boys hired me as a live-in housekeeper-babysitter for the summer. The boys were a handful and my skills with young children were not particularly spectacular. The next biggest challenge was cooking the evening meal. She always left me a complete menu for the meal and it always was a full meal: meat, potatoes in various ways, a vegetable, salad, bread and dessert. I liked to cook and was partially successful in preparing the meal, but I was not emotionally nor psychologically prepared for keeping a home, taking care of two very spoiled little boys and preparing a full evening meal along with a pie or cake or other beautiful sweet treat. I was also left to my own devices on my "off" hours after dinner and on weekends until I needed to be up in the morning to once again take up my assigned duties. I was woefully immature and completely unready to be on my own. The summer ended in ignominy as I partied myself into exhaustion and illness.

College and living in a college dormitory in 1952 was good for me. Dormitory life was not even close to what it is today. Boys were not allowed into the girls' dormitories and there were definite rules for going out in the evenings or weekends and when you needed to be back in the building. Meals for all students were held at specific hours in a dining hall and, of course, everyone ate whatever was served. As the College of Idaho was a Presbyterian school, there were religious influences in all the activities. One evening meal a week was rice only and the money saved was sent to the mission field. In the dormitories there were house mothers, adults who lived there and were available to students as well as making sure students were always chaperoned. Also each floor had upper class monitors to enforce rules and etiquette. However, it was still a heady experience and gave more freedom to choose your friends and activities. I soon found a part time job at the local Sears store. I worked as a salesperson, first in the shoe department and eventually in house wares. During the Christmas season, one of the secret customers, hired by Sears to shop and rate the quality of the salesperson helping them, bought a considerable amount of merchandise from me and I was given such a high rating that I kept my job after the holiday rush. That was a good thing, since I really needed the money. My folks were paying for school but I had to pay for myself.

The only class I really enjoyed was psychology. On the first day of class, I had been warned that the teacher would tell all freshmen to leave because he didn't take freshmen in his class. If you didn't get up and leave but simply stayed, you would be accepted. I believe one other freshman did the same thing as I did. I learned a lot in that class and was very glad I had the warning and advice. None of the other classes I took engaged me in the slightest. The only ones I even remember taking were English literature and Spanish. I did a mediocre but adequate job in those.

My main interest was the attention I got from several young men and the enjoyment I had from my job at Sears. My hours at work had increased and I found myself learning to eat quickly, if at all, and hurry, in order to get everything I had to do finished during the day. I started going out with a senior, Ray Vinson, from Boise, and we began spending considerable time together. He was majoring in Spanish and I enjoyed trying to have conversations with him in Spanish. He was very serious, although a bit bohemian, and we had some great conversations.

In late May a young man from Homedale, Warren Nanney, came to work at Sears as a TV repairman. He was taking electronics at Oregon Technical Institute in Klamath Falls, Oregon, and had to drop out of school with one term left because of financial difficulty. His intention was to work at Sears until fall and then go back and finish his schooling and be able to come back and work at Sears. Television was just getting to this part of Idaho and anyone with electronics education was in high demand. People were buying huge antennas and farmers from miles around were paying to be able to have television in their homes. Warren worked a lot of overtime and thrived on the excitement the new medium was bringing to people's lives. Warren told me that he liked watching me walk down the store aisle and so he decided to catch me and ask me out for a date. I didn't have a clue what he was talking about, but I liked the idea of a date.

For our first date Warren explained that his sister had just gotten married and the friends and family of the bride and groom planned a chivaree that night. I had never heard of this celebration but it became the first of a good many learning opportunities I had after being introduced to Warren's family. Today if one looks up chivaree on the internet there are as many traditions as there are cultures and regional differences. The one commonality seems to be the celebration by friends and family of a newly wed couple by noise, singing and various practical jokes and pranks to tease the couple and draw attention to their new sexual relationship. In its best light it was a noisy, boisterous and happy experience but on occasion these celebrations turned malicious and were not welcomed. The term doesn't even show up in the Merriam-Webster Collegiate Dictionary 10th edition. I suspect the huge sexual revolution which has taken place in the last years of the 20th century and early years of the 21st has taken its toll on traditions like the chivaree. There no longer exists, at least in most of the United States, the tradition that the bride is a blushing virgin who knows nothing about copulation nor is the groom always a macho, well experienced and ready-to-gently-teach male. The remnants of the chivaree, consisting of decorating the couple's car with "Just Married" or other comments and tin cans or other noisy attachments to the car, continue to be used. In many places, a long caravan forms to follow the bridal couple's auto when they leave their wedding or reception. Much honking and noise ensues for a lengthy period of time, depending on where the couple leads the parade.

Shivaree[1] is the most common American regional form of charivari, a word of French origin meaning "a noisy mock serenade for newlyweds." In the past, shivarees were given to married couples who were thought to be mismatched or to people whose conduct was considered scandalous. The French term probably derives from the Late Latin word meaning "headache," carībaria, which in turn is from Greek karēbariā, a compound of karē, "head," and barus, "heavy." English shivaree, most likely borrowed from French traders and settlers along the Mississippi River, was well established in the United States by 1805. The word shivaree is especially common along and west of the Mississippi River. Its use thus forms a dialect boundary running north-south, dividing western usage from eastern. This is unusual in that most dialect boundaries run east-west, dividing the country into northern and southern dialect regions. Some regional equivalents are belling, used in Pennsylvania, West Virginia, Ohio, Indiana, and Michigan; horning, from upstate New York, northern Pennsylvania, and western New England; and serenade, a term used chiefly in the South Atlantic states.

The shivaree I attended that June night for Warren's sister Margie and her new husband Leroy was good natured and noisy. The bride and groom were individually captured and put in separate cars which led the long parade of honking cars and trucks, with people hanging from all the windows, from the Nanney farmstead into

---

[1] American Heritage7 Dictionary of the English Language, Fourth Edition copyright 82000 by Houghton Mifflin Company. Updated in 2009. Published by <u>Houghton Mifflin Company</u>. All rights reserved

the small town of Homedale. There Margie was tumbled into a wheelbarrow and Leroy was directed with much razzing and shoving to pushing the wheelbarrow into the small movie theater and up and down the aisles, where the projector was turned off temporarily and everyone whooped and hollered, after which the movie was re-started. The noisy trespassers left the movie and the group left town, going their separate ways returning the happy couple home. While the crowd was in Homedale, another group short-sheeted their bed and filled the sheets with straw.

This was my introduction to Warren's family and life. He had five siblings, all married except for him. They were loud and boisterous with strong family ties, enjoyed family gatherings, eating, laughing and being together.

We had fun together, laughed a lot and went exploring Owyhee County, a large mostly unpopulated, hilly desert area. A lot of this area was being homesteaded and wells were being drilled for water for agriculture. We spent that summer together mostly doing outdoors activities. Many times we took a picnic and drove up Succor Creek, with Marge and Leroy, danced to the car radio in the middle of the road, and climbed the rocky hills to see what we could find. We would come home late at night, tired and frequently sun-burned but very happy. Most of the time these outings took place on weekends since both of us worked. I would frequently go home with Warren to Homedale on Friday evening and stay with his family over the weekend. That was a wonderful summer of 1953.

My dislike of peppermint started that summer. Warren worked a lot of overtime with the TV frenzy in full force and I would sit in his car and wait for him on Friday evenings. He was particularly late one weekend so I went over to the drug store and bought a box of chocolate peppermint patties because I was so hungry. I ate the whole box full! Warren's poor mother ended up holding my head all night long as I spent the night in the bathroom. I have never eaten peppermint since!

I had continued working at Sears when school was out in June. However, home life had become unbearable for me. It was probably unbearable for Elaine also, because I was definitely feeling very independent. In any event, Grandma Chapin had a fall and broke her hip and had been in the hospital for about a month. She contracted gangrene because the bone was not healing and died. Elaine and I had a mother-daughter teenage fight and I had left home to stay with a friend. I came home when Elaine contacted me about Grandma Chapin. When I walked in the door she charged up to me and told me that she had cleaned my room, that it needed to be kept clean or I would have to move out. I immediately packed my personal belongings and called Warren. We went apartment hunting for me. I found a small one room apartment in Caldwell and moved in. The landlord said she had a relative possibly coming to live with her and if that relative arrived, I would have to move. Since I needed a place to stay immediately, I took the apartment as offered. Many years later I am sure that she just wanted to check me out to be sure there wasn't a parade of men coming to visit me. She had a way to get rid of me from the beginning if that should happen.

Suddenly Don Carpenter came back into my life. The correspondence between us had tapered off until I hadn't heard from him for several months. We had visited once during this two year period of time. When I first started college at College of Idaho in Caldwell, I had taken a bus to Oklahoma City to visit him and then he came back to Nampa with me to meet my family. As an aside, that bus trip was an educational eye opener for me. The thing that struck me the most was seeing the signs: two water fountains for instance with a sign saying "Colored" on one of them. I had never realized what living in southern states meant. When I got home from that trip, my dad had the only talk I ever remember having with him. He advised me against being too serious about Don because he was a "Southern boy" and "Southern men do not always treat their women well." Having seen the segregation and discrimination against blacks on my visit, I was totally appalled and by the time we concluded our visit in Nampa our relationship was essentially ended. However, a few months later, I got a call at work from Elaine telling me that Don was in Nampa and wanted to see me. He arrived at the store shortly after the phone call and we went out to dinner after I got off work at 6. The discussion was brief but friendly and I asked for a day or so to think about it. We walked back to my apartment where, unbeknownst to me, Warren was waiting.

I introduced the two men and explained that I had asked Don for some time to think about the situation. Warren's comment was, "For me, she doesn't need any time. She can make up her mind here and now which one of us she wants." With that, he walked away and got in his car, which was parked in front. I started crying and Don tried to talk to me, but all I could say was "I think Warren is right, Don. I'm sorry." A few years later Warren and I were in Oklahoma City for FAA schooling. I looked up Don's parents, found his mother at home, and returned Don's class ring. She told me Don was in Salt Lake City, happily married, and heavily involved in the Mormon church.

After Don's visit, Warren and I spent that night talking about getting married. We went to Nampa the following day and told my folks that we were going to get married. Elaine immediately wanted to give us some money and let us go to the courthouse. Warren and I left Nampa and Warren went to Homedale to tell his parents. At work on Monday, Elaine phoned me and said that she and Daddy wanted to give me a wedding and asked if Warren and I could come over to talk about it for dinner that evening.

Doris Marie & Warren J Nanney

We settled on September 20th for the wedding, which was six weeks away. It was a mad scramble, but we managed to put it together. The only conundrum that occurred was over the wedding dress. The one I liked the best was the most expensive! I told Elaine that it was okay, the less expensive one was beautiful too. She called me a couple of days later and told me that I could have the more expensive one. It was a beautiful wedding and Grandma and Grandpa, Aunt Dot, Uncle Tom, Diane and my friend Barbara Farnworth from Blackfoot came over for it. The Bellingmos, Grandma and Grandpa's neighbors two doors down from them, also came. One of my high school formals fit Diane and she became a bridesmaid along with Donna Rookstool, a friend from college, who was maid of honor. Warren had two friends as groomsmen: Bob Price and Chuck Adams. I am still in touch with Bob Price's ex-wife but have lost contact with Chuck Adams. Warren and Chuck had been very close friends at Oregon Tech where they both went to school, but Chuck drifted away shortly after Warren and I were married. We were married at the Presbyterian Church in Caldwell and had a small but very nice reception at my folks' home in Nampa after the wedding. Warren's siblings, who were in the local area, all attended along with their families. Those included Bob and Dorothy, Junior and Helen and their girls, Edna and Irvin, and Marge and Leroy. Alice and Babe were living in Pocatello and were not able to come. Of course, Irene and Ivan, Warren's parents, came. For such a short time of preparation, it was a lovely wedding. Elaine was unhappy because she and Daddy were not invited to Irene and Ivan's home prior to the wedding. Elaine invited them to dinner and whatever rule of etiquette hadn't been followed was corrected as far as Elaine was concerned. Certainly Warren and I were not particularly interested in etiquette; we just wanted to be married and on with our lives. The men all wore nice suits as opposed to tuxedos. I don't remember any particular color scheme. Warren and I took off immediately after the reception for Klamath Falls, Oregon. Warren had business at Oregon Technical Institute where he had been going to school.

Of course, our car had been well decorated for us. Since it was late in the day, we didn't get very far before we looked for a motel to spend the night. All that was available in the one motel we found was a room with two beds. The landlady wanted $7 for the room with two beds. We didn't have much money but we were tired so Warren, who had been negotiating with her, walked to the door with her. She stepped outside, saw our car all decorated up with "just married" signs, threw her hands up in the air and said "Oh my goodness, newlyweds. Well, I guess I don't have to worry about you using both beds. You can have the room for $5." A few hours earlier we had stopped at a Chinese restaurant to eat (Chinese food was always the cheapest) and when we sat down in the booth, rice fell out of my hair all over the table and there was a to-do about just being married.

In Klamath Falls, Warren went to Oregon Tech to take care of some bills he had there and to let them know he was not coming back for the fall quarter. Our trip to Crater Lake consisted of driving around the lake in one day. We were gone on this "honeymoon" about three days altogether and then went home to get back to work.

Warren & Doris Nanney

There were about fifteen years when Warren and I, Marge and Leroy and Bob and Shareen Price were close friends and maintained close contact. We were

Doris Chapin Bailey

all married within months of each other, Marge in June, us in September and Bob and Shareen in October. Marge was pregnant when she and Leroy were married. She had gone to Edna who had taken her to the doctor for confirmation and then convinced their parents that the marriage date should be moved from August to June. From the hindsight of many years, I am convinced they knew. Leroy came pounding on our door at 2 a.m. on February 5th to announce they had just had a son. He was upset over having a "seven-month baby" as it was called back then. Warren and he talked for a long time until Leroy felt better. They ended up having five sons: Donald, Stephen, Philip, Jeffrey in 1960 and then a late son, Joshua, born in late 1971. Warren died on January 8, 1973, and Marge had been at our house for a couple of weeks or so, taking care of Warren, and missing Joshua's first birthday. They moved to Lesotho in Africa within a year or so of Warren's death. Roy and I were in Idaho visiting, and I went to see her. I have had very few close women friends over the years and the loss of Marge was very sad to me. She died on her birthday, January 31, 2008. Leroy went back to Nairobi where he stayed until 2011 when he moved to Caldwell, Idaho. I was able to visit with him a couple of times at Donna's home near Caldwell. Donna and her mother, Dorothy, had moved from California back to Idaho several years previously and Donna's has become the meeting place for various family visits since then. Leroy was killed by a car when he was walking from Caldwell to Donna's one evening for dinner.

Warren's and my first home was an upstairs apartment at 321 Aven Avenue in Caldwell. The house has since been torn down and is a used car lot. Both of us continued to work at Sears. Shortly after we were married Warren had the accident which left the scar on his nose. These were the early days of TV in Idaho. Warren was installing a very tall and heavy antenna on a house in the country. He had to climb up the base of the antenna to lift the antenna itself up and attach it to the base. It was like being on a ladder holding this heavy, tall (another 6-8 feet antenna) above the base and then lowering it into the base. He slipped and the pipe at the end of the antenna, about 1" in diameter came down and caught him squarely on the left side of his nose.

The people who lived in the house rushed him to the hospital, where they sewed him up. However, the sewing job was done very poorly and he had a terrible scar from it that never went away. I remember that he was late getting back to Sears, as usual, and I was waiting for him when the Manager of Sears came out and told me not to be alarmed but that Warren had been in an accident. I had to wait until he got back to Caldwell, since he was at some tiny town fifty or sixty miles away. I don't think he even missed one day of work.

Warren really wanted to finish his electronics schooling at Oregon Technical Institute, so he started talking to Sears about how to go about this. He only had but a single quarter left to get his diploma. Sears agreed to help him get his final quarter by having Warren haul to Klamath Falls a large piece of equipment for assisting in the installation of large, high antennas and the Sears store would hire Warren to work in their TV installation and maintenance department while he was going to school until he finished getting his diploma. Then we would come back to Caldwell and Warren would work for Sears in Caldwell again. Management in the Klamath Falls store was happy to have the equipment at no cost to them, but they put off hiring him until I started crying one day because we were down to practically no money and no food with the rent due again. We had rented a small apartment downtown, but finally got quarters up on campus which was cheaper for married students. The school was using old military barracks made into apartments for married students and was able to charge considerably less than market prices. We had been paying $50 a month downtown and the campus rates were $35. We had arrived in Klamath Falls with one-half of a lamb, frozen, a box of twelve packages of frozen peas and two dozen jars of canned peaches. We were living on that food during that first month. It was a tremendous financial relief to get moved onto campus. We were down to practically no money and had spent a whole dollar on a jig-saw puzzle for entertainment when Warren was finally put to work and got a paycheck. I found a job on campus working in the office as a temporary clerk.

My grandparents came to visit and see where we were living on one occasion while we were in Klamath Falls. We enjoyed the Klamath area and we spent much of the little spare time we had available exploring the countryside in our pickup with a homemade camper shell on the back where we could sleep. One time we decided to go see California. We filled up the gas tank (at eighteen cents per gallon) and drove south til we were almost down to one- half a tank of gas. We thought it might be fun to go back to Klamath via a different route. Warren spotted a policeman and went over to ask him if it was any farther to go back to Klamath that way. When the policeman found out we had one tank of gas and were just about down to one-half he told us to turn around and go back exactly the way we had come!

The other place I remember going to explore while we were in Klamath Falls was the Tule Lakes and Captain Jack's stronghold area. That was really fascinating to me and I enjoyed it a lot. In later years I learned that Roy had worked for Weyerhauser Timber in the same area during the summers and had also found the Captain Jack stronghold area interesting. All in all, those three months were fun. Warren got his diploma and we packed up a U-haul trailer with the used furniture we had bought in Klamath to go home to Caldwell.

We rented a house on Illinois Street out in the country. We loved that house with a big lot where we could have a garden. We went into partners with Edna and Irvin and bought 125 chicks. The deal was that I would take care of the chicks for six to eight weeks until they were ready to be killed and prepared for the freezer. Edna and Irvin were going to pay the costs involved and all four of us would then get together to put the chickens in the freezer. We had just barely bought the chicks and got everything set up okay when I got sick. I was so sick I went to see a doctor who gave me some kind of medicine which made me even sicker. I finally called Elaine, who came to get me to her doctor. The next thing I knew, Warren was there and I was getting a spinal tap. Elaine came in and told me the doctor didn't want to tell me what was wrong but she didn't agree with doing that because she felt someone who was sick needed to know what was wrong so they could be prepared mentally for what was happening. Warren agreed with her, so they told me I had polio.

I was taken by ambulance to Boise and I was a pretty sick person for about ten days. This was 1954, during the years of the polio epidemics. My cousin Diane was just recovering from a very severe case of paralytic polio. Neither of us lost the use of our lungs, so we were lucky. Once you got sick, the disease simply had to run its course and then they went to work on whatever you had left. During the course of the illness, some doctors used Sister Kenny's method of hot towels, others used penicillin, etc. All were simply guessing games, as they really didn't know what to do. My doctor put me on injections of penicillin, saying he didn't know if it would help, but it wouldn't hurt either. The thing I remember the most is the tremendous sensitivity of the skin. I couldn't stand anything, not even a sheet, to touch my skin. I ran a high fever, suffered nausea and violently hurt all over. Also I got extremely constipated. When my fever broke and I started feeling better, my right side was the part of me affected. Also my epiglottis was sluggish. I could still walk, but it was quite difficult and tiring, so I did spend some time in a wheelchair. My right arm didn't work at all. It was a very strange feeling to try to reach up to get something and not have my arm respond.

I was transferred to the Elks' Rehabilitation Hospital in Boise and they went to work to see what muscles could come back or what muscles could be retrained to do the job that muscles that were completely gone used to do. It was long and arduous, but slowly the muscles started regaining strength. My leg came back first but my arm took over a year's worth of physical therapy. First I was an inpatient at the Elks and then I went on an outpatient basis until the end of 1955. I continued to go to physical therapy once a week until I got pregnant in December of 1955. I have some very slight residual paralysis still.

My illness took quite a toll on our financial affairs. I was in Boise and Warren was working in Caldwell. He didn't work just eight hours daily; sometimes it was ten or twelve or more. TV was still the rage and everybody wanted it. The first thing Warren did after I got ill was to pack up all our belongings and move back to his parents' home in Homedale. It was impossible to pay the rent on the house on Illinois and drive back and forth to Boise to see me every day. Meals, hospital and doctor bills were completely out of our realm of income. March of Dimes helped us pay the doctor's bills and the Elks never charged us, because their charges were based on ability to pay. The insurance Warren had with Sears paid the hospital bill. I have always felt gratitude toward both the Elks and the March of Dimes because of the help we got at this time. This is also why I went to work as quickly as I could while I was recovering.

When I was finally released from the Elks I went to Homedale and we stayed there for a while. Warren worked with me every day with weights and exercising. I also had physical therapy every other day, driving back to Boise and then it tapered off to once a week. At that point we were able to find a duplex to rent on 10th Street in Caldwell and I went to work for Caxton Printers. Grandpa knew the elder Mr. Gipson, whose family owned Caxton Printers. Grandpa made the trip to Caldwell to check out what I was doing and how I was. He and Grandma also visited me while I was in the hospital.

It was also about this time that we took up our "desert claim." This was an Act of Congress that allowed a person to "claim" up to 360 acres of desert land. In order to secure a patent (deed) on it one had to 1. Get water to it, and 2. Cultivate and raise a crop. Living on it was encouraged but not necessary. The land we claimed was beautiful desert country, in a little valley, reasonably flat and excellent terrain for putting in a crop, with a couple of rolling hills that were perfect for home sites. There were one or two cases of very deep wells hitting artesian water, both hot and cold. We took every bit of money we had and bought a "well rig" and spent weekends, holidays and evenings out on our "claim" working. This began in the summer of 1954 when we returned from Oregon Tech and was then put on hold by my getting sick and was continuing into 1955 when we had a chance to buy our first home.

Warren's friend, Blanche (he had managed to get her a TV signal) owned a lot of real estate in Caldwell. They got to talking about Warren buying a house from her that she wanted to sell. Warren said, "Well, we'd like to have our own home, but we owe all this money on this well rig we bought." So they came up with a deal. Between the two of us we made $85 a week. For four months we saved $50 a week for every week except the week we paid our rent. In return Blanche paid off the well rig and took the pink slip on our pickup as collateral. At the end of four months we gave Blanche the $600 and signed a Contract of Sale for a house at 209 Elm Street, payable at $65 a month, 6% interest (high for those days) at a total price of $8,750. We paid off the loan on our pickup by continuing the $50 a week payments for another two or three months. Blanche used to laugh and tell people it's the first time she had to come up with cash herself in order to sell someone a house! The payments were $15 more per month than we were paying for rent but it was our very own house, which really meant a lot. We moved in late spring of 1955. The house had two bedrooms, bathroom, living room and kitchen. It also had a full basement with an outside entrance. It had an unattached single car garage on the side. It was one of those ticky tacky cracker boxes that were built right after WWII to try to fill the housing shortage with all the servicemen coming home. It had a big yard, raspberry bushes and a big area for a garden. Across the street was a pasture. There was an alley behind the house. We also had a grape arbor with wonderful Concord grapes on it. The yard had dahlias and peonies and the front was nicely landscaped with decorative conifers. It was a pretty place and we were very happy.

We continued to work on our desert claim, but hit solid rock about 200 feet down and could never afford to buy the rock bit necessary to drill through rock. We eventually had to let the claim go by 1958 when we left the state of Idaho, and, as it turned out, never returned to live there. At one time Junior tried to have it transferred to him, but there were some legalities that prevented it. It was reclaimed many years later and is now beautiful and valuable farmland.

In the meantime, I got pregnant in December of 1955. We were so happy and excited about finally having a baby. We had been trying since we were married in 1953 but with no success. Gayleen René was born on August 19, 1956. This was her great grandfather Andersen's 76th birthday. Then on February 5, 1958, her sister, Janice Diane, was born.

Warren started learning to fly before the girls were born. He first bought into a little Aeronca Champ with three others. As so often happens in cases like this, when the airframe certificate had to be renewed and the plane had to have the frame sanded and the fabric replaced, the others dropped out and we were left with buying the plane and repairing it. A good part of this work was done in our driveway. I soon learned what acetone smelled like.

Shortly after we were married we joined a group associated with civil defense. The country was still jittery from World War II and the Korean War and was keeping a sharp lookout for low flying planes encroaching on our airspace. Towns everywhere had civil defense lookouts who watched for any planes. The lookout in Caldwell was on top of the local hotel and we took our turn on watch once a week early in the morning. From the interest in planes and the civil defense work, we soon gravitated to the Civil Air Patrol, with its foundation in search and rescue operations. Eventually we both became officers and I became Commandant of the Cadets. We had a group of ten to twelve teenagers. We got a local National Guard colonel who wanted to get more credit toward his retirement benefits to teach a class on aerodynamics. I learned a lot from that class too. Several of our cadets earned national honors and awards and one of our group got to fly to Washington D.C. on a week long tour. We also took the kids out on simulated search and rescue operations in the desert. All in all, Warren got lots of flying time, which was his delight and I enjoyed working with the kids. We participated in SARCAPs all over Southern Idaho and flew by military plane to an Air Force base in Colorado one time for exercises. On one SARCAP in Idaho Falls I drove over to spend some time in Blackfoot and Warren flew his plane. There was such a head wind that he could see his shadow on the sagebrush below, barely creeping forward. It was so slow he only got to Burley and had to overnight there. He slept in the plane. He said the cars on the roads below were passing him. Both of us really enjoyed our CAP days. All this took place from 1954 through about 1957 when I became pregnant with Jan and I had to give something up. Warren kept his plane though and continued both in CAP and with his private flying. He never did progress far enough, however, to be able to take passengers aboard.

Warren's father died in February of 1956. He died at home and I don't know the cause of death. His mother decided to try to get enough credit through Social Security to get some income so she worked the orchard and kept the sheep. She rented out the crop land for cash. She had to have a certain number of quarters of paying into social security before she would be able to apply for benefits. She was only in her late 50's, with her only income through the farm. She had to keep on farming and hope by the time she was 62 she would be able to stop. She was living mostly on the cash rental. I doubt she had any other income unless there was a VA pension since Ivan was a World War I veteran. In any event, by 1958 she was in quite desperate straits, so Warren talked me into renting our house out and moving to Homedale to live with her so he could help her. He plowed a little air strip out of a hillside near the house and proceeded to fly back and forth to work at Sears. I have often thought the primary reason he wanted to move was the chance to fly. He loved flying. He said it was the only time he felt actually relaxed and at peace with himself and the world. He was able to fly until 1962, when the expenses were more than we could manage and he had to give it up. We sold the plane in Pendleton, Oregon. He was able to pursue flying for almost ten years. The final straw that broke the airplane owner's back was the FAA's requirement that all aircraft had to have air to ground communications. The world was progressing.

We moved into Irene's house and lived with her there for six months. Warren was still active with CAP because he wanted to be involved in search and rescue and also because he loved to fly. He had gotten a couple of the neighbor boys to join the cadets and was transporting them back and forth to meetings. This included one of Leroy Scherer's brothers and a friend of his. On one particular night he should have returned by 10 or 10:30. At midnight I called one of the CAP members in Caldwell and was told the meeting had dismissed at 9:30 and Warren had left. Apparently the operator had been listening in to the conversation. This was not uncommon back then especially on country phone systems like Homedale's. As soon as I hung up the phone rang. The operator said "I don't want to alarm you but there has been an accident between Caldwell and Homedale and there were some injuries taken to Caldwell hospital." I called the Caldwell hospital and found that yes, there had been a car accident and Warren and the two boys had been admitted. This was in the era before seat belts were required. Warren had a concussion and several stitches in his head, one of the boys broke an arm and the other boy had put his head through our girls' potty chair which had been sitting in the back seat. He also had three teeth broken. All three were sleeping and were in no danger so the hospital recommended we wait until morning to come over.

Warren was discharged in a couple of days and the boys were discharged a few days later. The other car's insurance paid all the medical bills and replaced our Triumph which was totaled. About an hour after we had finally located Warren in the hospital, we got a telephone call from someone who was at the scene of the accident and had been asked by someone to call us and was just getting around to it. We had to go to the boys' homes that night and let the parents know, because neither had a telephone. Irene was very supportive.

Irene always had trouble having her daughters-in-law living with her. Dorothy and Helen both had troubles with her. For some reason Irene would eventually begin to suspect her daughters-in-law of various misdeeds and start recounting said misdeeds to her sons. In each case this resulted in the son and daughter-in-law moving out and leaving her alone once again. According to Irene, Helen stole food, Dorothy tried to kill her cat and my misdeed was hiding her rubber boots. She insisted she had seen me do it through the bedroom window. Several weeks later we figured out what she had seen. I had a black purse with a long strap used to put the purse over the shoulder. When I had left that morning I was carrying it in my hand and it was hanging down about to the ground. We made a specific decision at that point to move as soon as possible.

We had rented out our house, so we went looking and found some people who were selling their 8' x 45' two-bedroom trailer. All we had to do was assume their loan. The sellers simply wanted to be out from under the debt. We moved into the trailer in July or August of 1958. Although Jan was only a few months old we needed additional money to meet living expenses, so I found a job at Mercy Hospital, which was Catholic. A nun was in charge. I worked there as the insurance and admissions clerk. I rather liked the job, but I was only there three months when Warren received a job offer from the Civil Aeronautics Agency to join them as an electronics tech in Great Falls, Montana. We packed everything up and began the first of several moves with our trailer (now known as mobile homes but back then they were trailers, no matter what size.) By this time Warren had worked for Sears for five and a half years.

We arrived in Great Falls, Montana, on December 22, 1958. It took about a week to make the move, which went very well. It was a good thing we had two four-day weekends in a row after we first got there, because we were not accustomed to the bitter cold east of the Rockies. It took us both four day weekends to get the trailer winterized. We used 50 gallons of oil a week and I kept the girls in snowsuits inside the trailer. We could get the temperature up to only 60 degrees with the furnace running non-stop. There was ice about 2" thick on the inside of the windows. The sewer drain froze up and the manager of the trailer court and Warren worked for several hours to get it unplugged. The only way was by reaching in and pulling everything out. Some kids had thrown rocks down the opening and plugged it up. Anyway, we had to close off the bottom of the trailer and put bales of straw under the trailer for insulation. Then on the inside of the windows we used a vacuum cleaner turned backwards to blow and melt the ice off the windows, sop the water with towels and then quickly cover the windows with clear visqueen and masking tape to make storm windows. We had a big wind storm one night before we were finished and it blew some of our sheets of corrugated metal away, but, we found them and were still able to use them. What country! We really had a time with the cold. When the wind blew you could see our trailer walls move in and out. On Christmas Eve Warren went out to find a tree and found a two foot high one that had three or four branches on it. We decorated and had a good Christmas anyway, our first away from Idaho.

The only other thing of any consequence that I remember about Great Falls was the big Ice Storm. Warren called me from work one day to say he could look out from the airport tower and see a huge white wall advancing toward Great Falls. It covered the entire horizon. He warned me not to leave the trailer for any reason. The temperature dropped from 30 degrees F. to 60 degrees below zero in two hours. I could watch the thermometer go down. For two solid weeks after that, the highest it got during the middle of the day was 15 degrees below zero. When the temperature went up to 20 degrees above zero it was like we were having a heat wave. We made a trip out to some natural hot springs and it was beautiful. The steam from the water had caused all the trees and bushes to be completely molded in ice and everything looked like ice sculptures with the steam rising from the pools. This was also where I learned that the Missouri River came up through Montana, which was a big surprise to me.

Everyone said we would love it in the summer, but the winter was so severe and we were so uncomfortable in the bitter cold that we decided we really didn't want to stay there. When Warren was scheduled for Communications Equipment School, which all new technicians had to take as soon as possible after being hired, we packed up everything and hoped we would not be back.

When we were getting everything ready to leave, there was a chinook wind. A chinook wind is a warm wind blowing in on the frozen earth and the top portion begins to melt, leaving the layer of ice underneath so everything is very slippery. We had our trailer jacked up. I was downtown trying to get the insurance straightened out. George and Ginny Wilkes were visiting and were watching the girls when the trailer slipped off the jacks. Fortunately no one was hurt, but I don't know why they weren't. All my dishes on the overhead shelves fell off and broke, the refrigerator door came open and everything spilled out on the floor and there was a horrible mess to clean up.

This was also when we had our first problem with State Farm Insurance. Warren had the accident with the car that landed him in the hospital and a couple of months later we were rear ended by some poor man who was so blind he couldn't read a billboard right beside the road. Gayleen was thrown from the back seat over the front seat and into the dashboard. Otherwise, everything was okay. She was okay too, but we had her checked over. Both the drivers in these two accidents were insured by State Farm and they paid the claim quickly and took good care of us. A friend of ours was a State Farm agent and we decided, "Gosh, they are really great insurance carriers" so we switched from Allstate to State Farm. Sometime between the time we left Idaho and were ready to leave Montana for Oklahoma City, State Farm cancelled our auto policy. This was back when the insurance company didn't have to notify the policy holder or even tell him why he was being cancelled. The insurance company could just do it and that's what they had done. We still don't know how long we had been driving around without insurance. I found out when I went down to get the trailer put back on the policy for moving on the road and found out there was no policy to put it back on. I spent one whole day trying to get auto insurance and no one would insure us. When I sat down in an insurance office and started crying the agent felt so sorry for me he said, I'll write you a policy to cover you until you reach Oklahoma City but as soon as you get there find somebody else to take you because I know once the company gets this application they will reject it." So that's how we managed to have insurance coverage while we made this move. Thank heavens we had no problems making the move. From that time for the next ten years we had trouble getting insurance. Finally in 1968 when we were in Capitola the AAA agent heard our story and insured us. Apparently, AAA allowed agents to make value judgments on things like this and he was able to write us a policy. This was about the time the film "2001, A Space Odyssey" came out and we spent a lot of time talking with him about the film. He also came over one time with a unicycle and showed us how he rode it. He was a very nice young man and we enjoyed him; apparently he enjoyed us too. We stayed with AAA until we moved to Alaska.

The truck we used to pull the trailer was an old bakery truck. It always caused a lot of conversation. Warren drove the truck and pulled the trailer and I drove the car. We traded off with the girls and later with all three children. We had our freezer, washer and dryer in the truck and used it like a utility room whenever we were parked. During these years mobile homes were truly mobile and lots of people used them as we did. Finding a space to park was usually not a huge problem and it was nice to always have a familiar home even if the surroundings were different. By the time we moved to San Jose, California, things were changing and mobile homes were getting larger and less mobile and finding a space was more and more difficult because of the decreased mobility and changes in zoning laws in various communities.

We got away from Great Falls early one morning after getting all the problems fixed caused by the jacks slipping and having no insurance. We almost got to Billings, Montana. This part of Montana is high plains country. You can see forever; the road consists of rolling hills, up, up one and then down, down to the next up, up. The topography is gentle undulating ground where they grow winter wheat. We soon discovered we were sixteen miles from Billings usually, because of the number of times we drove back and forth between Billings and where we were stranded. We first thought it was a head gasket but when that was replaced, we still had no power. Warren pulled the head and we took it into Billings, where we found an International garage who ran a double shift. When they tested the head it wouldn't hold any pressure at all. We talked them into letting us get the truck into town, parking in their alley and stringing an extension cord out to the truck so Warren could do the work. They wouldn't take anything but cash, however, and we didn't have enough cash. We had money in the bank but couldn't get to it. This was before widespread use of credit cards, so we telegraphed my parents saying, "Broken down in Billings, Montana. Need $100 for two weeks." They sent us the $100, but we sure caught heck later for sending a telegram instead of telephoning because they were worried about what was happening.

By the time we had made all the arrangements to get the truck fixed it was late afternoon and the sun had melted the frozen shoulder where we had parked. We were solidly stuck in the soft dirt. All day long not a single person had stopped to ask if they could help us which was quite unusual back when people were still mostly helpful. I finally flagged a farmer down in his pickup truck. He sauntered back to look things over and was highly skeptical about pulling us. He finally agreed, mostly because he was sorry for us, but he got us unstuck and back on the highway. However, we still didn't have sufficient power to make it on our own. The farmer agreed to stay with us but he would only pull us to the top of each hill. Then he would disconnect and let us coast downhill, where he would reconnect and pull us up the next hill. The sixteen miles to Billings turned out to be fifteen hills.

The International garage's second shift lasted until somewhere around midnight. Warren got through putting in the new head and getting it hooked up. Then he finished up in the morning after they opened up. We were able to get going again by noon.

The next adventure on this move happened in Casper, Wyoming. We always tried to stop somewhere for the night where we could hook up to electricity and have bathrooms. The best place was a service station. When we got to Casper it was late and very cold. I was tired and the girls were tired and we were all hungry. As usual, after Warren got the electricity hooked up he wanted to visit with the station attendant. I wanted to get the stove lit and get some food cooked. I tried to get the oil wall heater started for heat. It backfired at me and apparently covered me with soot although I didn't realize it at the time. I went charging into the station mad as a wet hen hollering for Warren to quit his visiting and help me get the stove lit. He thought I looked funny and laughed loudly. He did come in and get the stove going. After it was all over I could see how hilarious I must have looked and could laugh too, but at the time I was a whole lot angrier than I was amused.

The rest of that trip to Oklahoma City was fairly uneventful. We had to write ahead to all the states for "trip permits." Each state had different rules regarding length and width for highway vehicle travel. We were okay weight-wise for all states, but some considered us over length. Every time we crossed a state border we had to get new paperwork done. When we traded our 8 x 45 trailer for a 10 x 50 we had the problem of over-width too. We had looked into the requirements for each state before we left, so we were prepared.

We got to Oklahoma City and found a place to park while we were there at a motel way out the road south towards Norman. There were spaces for two trailers, the motel and six small cottages. There was a big empty field next to us. The motel had a swimming pool which was available to us and most of the tenants were Civil Aeronautics Agency people. This was the happiest trip we made to Oklahoma City during Warren's tenure with the CAA. The schooling was intense but interesting and Warren did reasonably well in it. CAA/FAA schools were always difficult and a lot of people had trouble, even those with college degrees in electronics. The math was strictly upper level college math and very specialized. It was not uncommon for graduate engineers to flounder in these schools. All the years with the FAA, both with Warren, and later with Roy, were spent going to school at least once each year and frequently more often. The schools differed in length from two weeks to nine months duration. In later years the FAA tried to have schools located locally, so there wasn't the jet lag and travel expenses involved for those who lived farther from Oklahoma. In those early years the Oklahoma City Federal Aviation Administration Academy was the only location available and those schools were mandatory, both for attendance and passing the course work.

We were there for Communications Equipment School between March and June 1959, so it was a pleasant time of the year temperature-wise. It was tornado season, which was especially worrisome to those of us who had never lived where tornadoes were a fact of life. The girls loved the swimming pool and became real water babies. With water ski belts around their waists they could jump off the edge to paddle around. They did so with gusto. Jan was a year old and Gayleen was 2-1/2. We had a close friendship with a man from Puerto Rico whose family ties were New York Italian. He was at school without his family and missed them ferociously. Carl Rosati and Warren studied together and the friendship continued down the road to another school. Since the last time we were in Oklahoma for school, Carl had accepted a job teaching at the academy and therefore he brought his family to Oklahoma. We were able to get to know his wife and children. It was from Carl that I got the spaghetti sauce recipe which I use to this day.

Warren investigated the possibility of changing duty stations as we had been so miserable in the bitter cold of Great Falls. We knew that in order to do this we would have to operate somewhat outside the regular channels, possibly faced a reprimand and undoubtedly would have to choose another "undesirable" station. He connected with Al Lincoln in Needles, California, where the temperature was 120 in the shade and there was no shade. However, in the winter it was 70 and the desert can be beautiful in the winter. Most important to us, it was west of the Rockies. We were not happy with the huge dose of weather extremes suffered by the Great Plains states east the Rockies: Montana, Kansas, Oklahoma. Through Al Lincoln Warren arranged a transfer directly from CE School to Needles, California. He did receive a reprimand, but it was a letter only and was purged from his records three years later.

The move to Needles was via the old Route 66, which had a certain amount of fame, including a TV series called "Route 66." This used to be the main east/west highway across the southern part of the USA connecting to Chicago. We found it a scenic and memorable trip. I especially remember Albuquerque and how it is nestled at the base of the mountains in a lovely valley. It was a very picturesque city. Our one adventure was on the long uphill haul out of Albuquerque toward Flagstaff. About two in the morning, the hardest part of the day for me when we were making these marathon moves, I realized that this uphill slog was going to go on for miles and miles, limiting Warren's progress pulling the trailer. I decided this was going to be a good time for me to pull off the road and take a nap since I could easily catch up with him later. I signaled Warren to stop, jumped out of the car, ran up to the truck and told him I was going to take a nap while he chugged up the mountain. I always drove with the doors locked, had left the keys in the ignition, and when I got back to the car I was locked out. Warren was already out of sight. I started pounding on the car windows trying to get the girls to wake up. After fifteen or twenty minutes I got Gayleen awake but couldn't get her to understand how to pull up the lock on the door and unlock it. I finally was able to flag down a car and asked them to please stop my husband up ahead and have him come back with the extra set of keys. When he was flagged down he had to drive several miles further to find a place big enough to get turned around. In the meantime, I was back at the car window trying to get Gayleen to unlock the door. She tried and tried, but didn't seem strong enough to lift the lock. Additionally, she was tired and cranky. She finally got the lock up and I was able to jump into the car, tell the girls to go back to sleep and rush up the road trying to catch Warren. Of course, I didn't catch him until after he was already on the way back down this mountain. Then he had to find another spot to turn around in and start crawling back up the mountain. Needless to say, he was a bit put out at all these shenanigans on a steep mountain road, no less." I never did get my nap.

Route 66 from Flagstaff drops from about 5500 feet to sea level, where Needles is located on the Colorado River very near where Nevada's tip points down toward Arizona on the east side of the river with California on the west side. Needles was a dusty, three block long typical desert town. The service stations did a brisk business during the summer gouging the tourists whose cars didn't tolerate the heat. There were signs reading "Hell - 2 feet ↓" Actually, in July and August I don't think you need two feet to reach it. It was possible to get burns if you tried to walk in the sand by the river during the summer. What all this meant was that during the summer no one went outside any more than was absolutely necessary. Lots of things were done at night including hanging out your wash to dry. A lot of the FAA technicians did their work early in the morning or late in the evening since some of the sites, even with refrigerated air cooling could get so hot there were cases of heat stroke among them. There was lots of work needing to be done because that old tube type equipment would suffer and break down if it got too hot. It was during our Needles year, I believe, that the Civil Aeronautics Agency changed its name to the Federal Aviation Agency. In the 1970's the name changed from Agency to Administration.

The first trailer court we tried to live in didn't have sufficient amperage for our air conditioning, so we located a little shack which was little more than a shed and the owner let us ostensibly rent the shack and park our trailer on the land next to it. It was right next to another trailer whose owners were doing the same thing. We dug a pit for our sewage, which worked fine because of the climate and topography, which was pure sand farther down than we could dig. We ran the water line over and did some modifications on the electricity and, voila! We had a home! We thought it was a pretty deserted town until fall when it cooled down some and everyone came out of the woodwork. Over time we planted a lawn and things were quite homey. We were in Needles for thirteen months and it was a good year.

Our next door neighbors were Fran and Augie Sullivan. He worked on the railroad, as did most of the longtime citizens in Needles. The railroad was essentially the reason for Needles' existence. Augie brewed his own beer. It was a compromise with his wife, who had threatened divorce because he had spent so much time in the bars downtown. She agreed that if he stayed home and brewed his own beer and drank it at home, she would stay with him. In the year we lived there he lived up to his word. They had two children, a son who had already left home and a daughter who was about twelve when we lived there. I enjoyed visiting with Fran and they were good neighbors.

We learned about date palms while in Needles. There were lots of date palms and anyone living there could get all the dates they wanted by just picking them. Of course, that took some doing! All our families received dates that Christmas! It was also the first time I had seen cotton growing - not at Needles but in some irrigated areas near there. We learned about the giant yucca and Joshua trees and the thousands of varieties of blooming cactus and wild flowers that spring up spontaneously in the spring. The hills were barren and rocky and had a strange and stark beauty. The summers were truly atrocious, but the other three seasons were pure heaven.

We also learned about flash floods. Warren and Al Lincoln were on their way to one of their sites when a flash flood hit. Al knew better, having lived there for many years, but he tried to go through one ravine where the water was running over the road. Roads are built with dips in them specifically for that purpose, to keep the water contained and directed. Longtime residents know that if there's been heavy rain in the hills and water is running across the road in a ravine, it's best to wait and not try to cross the running water. Al miscalculated the depth of the water, which is very easy to do and the water picked their station wagon up and they started going with the current. Warren climbed into the back and bracing his back against the back of the seat he used his legs and feet to smash out the back window. As they floated near one side of the gully they jumped out and scrambled up the bank. They picked cactus thorns out of their hands for weeks. Then they had to walk back to police lines, which had formed in order to be there to help those who had also made the mistake of trying to cross the running water, to get someone to take them back to town. A few days later they went down the gully and found the station wagon completely wrecked filled with gravel and other debris. They would never have lived through it if they hadn't gotten out when they did. This happened the first part of September, 1959. I was in Idaho at the time.

We had gone home to Idaho for a vacation about the middle of July. I was pregnant with John. It felt good to be where it wasn't so hot, although I laugh at that now, because I consider Idaho too hot in the summer. It was a lot cooler than Needles, however, so that was good. After Warren spent a couple of weeks he went back to Needles, but I stayed on with the girls. By this time I was having morning sickness and the thought of all that heat along with morning sickness was not a pleasant thing.

At the exact same time as the flash flood in Needles there was an over eight by the Richter scale earthquake in Yellowstone Park. I was sleeping in the front bedroom of my folks' house in Nampa and I was in that half asleep mode when you think odd things and I thought, "My gosh, Daddy is sure rocking in the rocking chair hard." Then I heard Daddy shout "earthquake." I jumped out of bed and ran to the living room, where things were definitely rocking and rolling. It lasted a couple of minutes. We were 350 miles from Yellowstone. We don't hear much about that big quake these days, but it did a huge amount of damage. None of it involved large cities so it didn't get the press. However, a whole mountain top slid off and completely buried a camp ground under a hundred feet of dirt, trees and rocks. They will never know for sure exactly who was there and who was buried there. It also completely changed the mud pots where brightly colored muds bubbled and boiled when I was a child. Some geysers were activated and others became dormant. Old Faithful remained faithful and the park remains one of the most visited in the country.

I had visited Yellowstone many times as a child and Warren and I and the girls had visited Yellowstone the summer of 1958 after Jan was born, so we had seen it before the earthquake. My grandparents, whom we visited on the way to the Park, were concerned about us planning to camp out, so they gave us money with instructions to rent a cabin, which we did. We spent four days in Yellowstone and had a wonderful time hiking all the trails and exploring everywhere. We even saw the Steamboat Geyser, which only spouts about once a month and cannot be timed, since it does not have a regular cycle like Old Faithful does. It spouts for about fifteen minutes and shoots the water out almost like a cannon and makes a sound like a steamboat, which is what gave it its name. We were fortunate to get to see it. Since we had visited Yellowstone the summer before the quake, we recognized all the place names mentioned in the various news reports. The earthquake was so much in the news because of Idaho's location in reference to Yellowstone that we didn't hear about the flash floods in Needles. Warren's mother Irene phoned the following morning from Homedale to say she had heard that Needles was under water. I immediately phoned and got Warren, learning about his and Al's brush with the flash flood, and that part of Needles was under water. However, where we were located was okay.

While I was in Idaho I did a huge amount of canning. I had always done a lot of canning every year living in Idaho: peaches, pears, tomatoes, applesauce, cherries, apricots, green beans, corn, asparagus, pickles and then relish, tomato sauce and all kinds of berry jellies and preserves, especially strawberry and raspberry. I went to the cannery in Homedale, which was marvelous because they had big tables and live steam available to scald your produce. Everything was packed into cans and then loaded onto trays on a conveyor belt. All your cans were marked with a grease pencil using your assigned code number so you could claim your cans after they were processed. The charge was so much per can, with different can sizes being different prices. It was a little more expensive than doing it at home, but so much quicker and easier that I always enjoyed it. I used the cannery from 1956 until I quit canning when we moved to California. Prior to 1956 I did all my canning at home. By the end of August that summer of 1959 I had put up about 300 cans of various produce. Warren called and wanted me to come home as he had to go to school for two weeks in El Centro, California, a little town about in the middle of California's border with Mexico. I packed up the car, the girls and my sister-in-law Marge and I took off for Needles. We drove straight through - twenty hours. One long desert stretch we thought we were going to run out of gas before we found a gas station, so we were putting the car in neutral and coasting down every incline to save gas when we finally got to a station.

When we got to our trailer, we discovered Warren had not done a good job of cleaning up after himself in the kitchen and all the crumbs had attracted sugar ants. So after twenty hours of driving Marge and I spent about four hours cleaning up so we could get rid of the ants, since we were leaving that night for El Centro. Marge took the bus back to Idaho and we went to El Centro for two weeks. While there Jan and Gayleen came down with whooping cough and Jan spent a night in the hospital, but both girls recovered just fine. We had a good time with the instructors in the course Warren was taking. Another interesting point about El Centro was the crickets! They had an infestation of crickets that was unbelievable. You couldn't walk down the sidewalk without stepping on them. They were everywhere, including the hospital, where employees were working diligently to get rid of them, but couldn't. We also spent the one weekend (daytime only) going into Mexicali in old Mexico. The thing I remember the most is that all the houses were painted in pastel hues of the rainbow. I got the impression that the people truly enjoyed colors. We didn't have any money so we didn't buy anything, we just wandered around and looked. Warren always liked to tell the story about looking through the viewfinder on his camera when he smelled a very strong sweet perfume waft under his nose. When he looked around to see who belonged to the perfume he saw two Mexican women in very tight short skirts smiling at him. He beat a quick retreat back to the car. El Centro was a little cooler than Needles and much larger.

When we lived in Needles we made at least one trip to San Jose to visit Alice and Babe and her family. It was very expensive to live in Needles, especially groceries. I remember that hamburger was 77 cents a pound there and most everywhere else it was 25 to 30 cents a pound. When we went to San Jose we bought a carload of meat and put dry ice with it. We laughed about it afterwards because when we left San Jose it was all fresh unfrozen meat. We drove through the desert heat to Needles and by the time we got there the meat was frozen. There was even some dry ice left. Our worries about whether we had enough to keep the meat from spoiling were not necessary.

We also made several trips to Los Angeles. These were the days before Los Angeles was routinely called L.A. We visited Knotts Berry Farm and Marineland and usually the FAA Regional Office. We didn't go to Disneyland because we wanted the kids to be old enough to really appreciate it before we went. I remember driving through Twenty Nine Palms on the way to LA, because there was a right angle left hand turn in the highway. If you missed the turn, the road straight ahead was gravel. Warren missed it one time when he was too tired to be driving and sure woke up in a hurry when he hit the gravel.

Needles was where I caught the first Asian flu to hit the U.S. I was so sick I didn't know which end was up. I remember making Gayleen and Jan play in the bedroom on the floor next to the bed so I could watch them because I couldn't get up. Anyway, it seemed to give me some immunity because I haven't gotten any of the Asian strains as badly as other people have since then.

In Needles we made two sets of friends. Ray Nelligan and his wife, Taka, replaced Al Lincoln a few months after we arrived there. We really enjoyed the Nelligans a lot. They did not have children and really enjoyed ours. In fact, a few years later they took the three children to Seaworld. We put the kids on a plane in San Francisco and Ray and Taka picked them up. They got a motel right on the beach and went to Seaworld for a couple of days and the kids had a glorious time. That's where Gayleen and Jan got their pearls that have been in the safety deposit box for so long.

The other set of friends were Gail and Ed Hawley. They had two girls exactly the same age as Gayleen and Jan. We became extremely close to them and remained close until about 1967 when we heard they were having marital problems, were considering divorce and Ed went to Alaska to be a bush pilot. We tried a couple of times to contact them after that without success. Ed worked for El Paso Gas, the second largest employer in the Needles area after the railroad. They lived in company housing outside town a ways. Ed was absolutely nuts about flying and would do almost anything to be able to fly. While we were in Needles Warren got our plane from Idaho and brought it down there, so he and Ed spent lots of hours flying. When we left Needles and moved to Pendleton, Oregon, Ed and Gail helped us move. We were quite a convoy headed north: Warren pulling our trailer home, me pulling a small baggage trailer, Gail in their car with their girls and Ed flying our plane!

We rotated visiting each other's houses, playing pinochle, visiting and going on picnics, etc. Since they were as broke as we were, we ate lots of meatless macaroni and tomato sauce. The girls got along fine.

One anecdote I often tell about our year in Needles was the experience of the big "bug." As I mentioned before, when the weather was hot, a lot of activity was conducted at night, when it was cooler. This was particularly true of laundry. When John was born I usually did the baby laundry at night and hung it out after dark, when it would dry very quickly. One night I went out shortly before dark and hung out a big load of baby things, mostly diapers. Warren went to a service station nearby for some reason and I went back out to gather in the dry laundry. I just gathered everything in my arms, took it back through the trailer to the back bedroom, which was ours, and threw it on the bed. Then I did some other chores and went back to fold the laundry.

When I walked to the back bedroom, there was a huge "something" flying up and down the rear wall. I closed the door quickly and ran over to Fran and Augie's house. Fran came back with me and we tiptoed back and peeked in the door. It was still flying up and down the back wall. I grabbed the broom and Fran stood guard by the door to make sure it stayed in that back bedroom. In our trailer the living room was in the front, then the kitchen, then the kids' room, where they were all asleep, then the bathroom, and then our bedroom. There was no hall. You simply walked through each room to get to the next. While Fran guarded the door, I ran to the phone and called the service station, where Warren was supposed to be. I got him on the phone and was trying to emphasize that he had to come home immediately - no delays. I said "This huge bug is flying up and down in our bedroom and it's as big as a can opener." The object in my mind's eye was the manual can opener attached to the kitchen wall in our kitchen. Of course, the term "can opener" could have many connotations, so Warren laughed and laughed and said he'd be right home. When he got home Fran and I were standing guard and Warren went into the back bedroom, where he laughed even more, bringing out and freeing a poor, helpless and frightened bat, which must have been tangled up in the laundry when I brought it in, and which was undoubtedly much relieved to find itself back in its own environment.

In the meantime, I was pregnant in the desert for the winter, so got lots of teasing about being barefoot and pregnant. I had a reasonably good pregnancy, although it was different from the girls'. I carried this baby lower, was more uncomfortable and soon learned the baby was breech. I was also severely anemic. Since we couldn't afford the vitamins I needed, the doctor was concerned and gave me Vitamin B complex shots, which were horrible things. He kept working to manipulate the baby, trying to get him to turn and about two days before the birth he did turn. One of the fellows Warren worked with and his wife had agreed to take the girls when I went into labor. I started labor on Warren's birthday, March 11th. A big party had been planned for his birthday and he ended up going to it by himself. We were kind of tickled, thinking that I was going to have this baby on his birthday and then labor stopped. Completely. The doctor said he wanted me to walk. We walked and walked. Finally, the next afternoon we decided to walk to the post office, which was up a hill thinking the uphill walk would surely start something. I got about halfway up and had to sit down and Warren went for the car. When I did go to the hospital about 7 p.m., things moved rather quickly. When the nurses asked how long I was in labor with the girls and I said "eighteen hours or so" they said, "oh well, this is a ways away then." However, that was not the case. They finally called for the doctor and Warren told me he hit the front door on a dead run. John Ellis Nanney was born March 12, 1960, at about 10:30 p.m. Ellis was, of course, my father's name and the only boy my father had as a descendant. He had, at the time of his death in 1988 only six granddaughters: Gayleen, Jan, Cory, Melany, Yong Hee and Michelle. John was his only grandson. Ellis was also Warren's father's middle name. The John was for Warren, whose middle name was John. So John was named for both his grandfathers and his father. My father always had a special place in his heart for his namesake.

This was the only time I suffered from post partum blues. They kept me in the hospital for almost four days. I missed the girls and the hospital wouldn't let them come in. I finally brought myself around after a couple of weeks. In July, Warren bid on Pendleton, Oregon, and thirteen months after arriving in Needles we were on the move again. Knowing the long hours of driving that moves of this type meant, I weaned John before we left Needles. When Gayleen was born I had inverted nipples and had a terrible time breast feeding, even to the point of bleeding. I finally succeeded and breast fed her until she was six months old. I got pregnant with Jan when Gayleen was nine months old. I breast fed Jan until she was six months old and had an easier time of it.

The convoy has been described that headed north from Needles. It was quite a trip and took about three days. We didn't travel around the clock because of the airplane. When we got to Idaho we parked at the Nanney farm and stayed there a few days before going on to Pendleton. This also gave us a chance to visit my family before going on.

While we were in Idaho there was a very bad wind storm that devastated the trees around the Nanney home. Our trailer was buried under fallen trees, as was the Hawley's car, but miraculously nothing was damaged. Altogether there were over twenty trees felled just around the house. The orchard also suffered some losses. The saddest loss was a gigantic Russian olive tree that had graced the front lawn of the house for longer than Ivan and Irene had owned the property, which was purchased in approximately 1926. There should be pictures among our belongings, showing the big tree with all the grandchildren sitting in it after it was down. It was a big job getting it cut up and removed. Although Irene had a fireplace, it was unused. I don't remember what happened to the wood. Gail was in the house watching the kids. I was away doing something or other. She heard the wind and put John on the floor and turned the recliner upside down on top of him. Then she took the four girls and got inside of a door frame with them, her mind was saying "tornado." Afterwards it was difficult to determine if it was a tornado, but it is quite possible since Idaho has records of having this type occasionally. However, they also frequently have simply strong wind storms. No structural damage or injuries occurred. It was very localized and did not affect anything beyond the immediate vicinity, perhaps one-half mile diameter.

We arrived in Pendleton, Oregon, in July 1960 and lived there until the end of December 1962, approximately two and a half years altogether. On our first arrival there we lived in a trailer court near the Umatilla River. When we returned from a stint in Oklahoma City for school, we moved into the trailer court up on the airport hill.

During our time in Pendleton we started attending the Christian Science church. Warren preferred it because that was the one he had grown up in. This was where we met Howard Baker who became a friend of ours. He and his wife and sons and son's families ran a dude ranch up the Umatilla River. They had a natural hot spring swimming pool, rustic cabins, a main ranch house, hiking trails and lots of horses for horseback riding. They also took groups hunting in the fall. We stayed in touch with Howard over the next ten years and he visited us in California after we left Pendleton.

We also became very close friends with Mid (Mildred) and Jack Eastep. Jack was the "electro-mech" for the FAA. He was an ex-Navy man who had played trumpet in the Navy band. They had three daughters, the youngest of which was a couple of years older than Gayleen. Of all the friends we had, we were the closest with Jack and Mid. I say this because we truly loved both of them. With many couples with whom we were friends at that time, it was one or the other of the two that was close to us, but with Jack and Mid, it was both of them. One of our saddest times was upon their deaths. In 1964 when we were in San Jose, California, Jack went over to the coast from Pendleton to check out a place they were thinking of buying, suddenly took ill and was rushed to the hospital. Mid called and the doctors told her Jack was okay and probably would be out in a day or two so not to rush over. A couple of hours later they called to tell her he had died. She was devastated. We never did get the entire story straight; they were devout Catholics, but about six months later Mid committed suicide. We tried to keep in touch with the girls for a few years, but lost touch with them eventually. It was a terrible loss.

In Pendleton we were living quite close to Edna and Irvin Hardiman and were able to visit with them quite frequently. It was only a couple of hours' drive to their farm near Royal City, Washington, where Irvin had won the opportunity for some land in a lottery for veterans a few years prior to our arrival in Pendleton. It was also while we were there in Pendleton that Bob and Dorothy were divorced, which rocked the family since there had been no divorces up to that time. Tommy came up for two summers in a row and spent most of the summer with us, which we enjoyed. We laughed because he wanted to go into electronics and Warren said he'd rather use a screwdriver than read the book. At this time, Tom has worked in electronic repair for many years and been successful.

We were very close to Edna and Irvin. Edna was the one who taught me so many things: how to cut up a chicken, how to make jam and jelly, how to can fruits and vegetables, how to bake bread and how to make many different recipes. I have several recipes in my recipe box in her handwriting. When we moved to Pendleton we were once again close enough to them to visit regularly. We shared costs of corn feeding some steers for the freezer and when we picked fruit for canning. I have many happy, warm memories of Edna, Irvin and their children.

Gayleen went to kindergarten and half of first grade in Pendleton. We still had Smokey, a mixed breed Australian sheep dog type which we had gotten in Caldwell after we bought our house on Elm Street. By this time Smokey was about five years old and Warren had spent a lot of time training him. Smokey was killed on our first tour in Oklahoma City from Pendleton in the fall of 1961. Most of the electronic techs had been upgraded from GS-7's to GS 9's but now the FAA was going to require nav-aid training and an upgrade to GS-11.

On this move we had two significant "adventures." On an empty straight road in the high plains country of Wyoming I was following the trailer and a radiator hose broke. To make a long story shorter, I was out there for about four hours. It was about an hour before someone came by that I could flag down and ask to stop my husband up ahead and tell him what had happened to me. Then a man stopped who worked somewhere out in that empty wilderness. He went to town back the way we came from, because in the direction we were headed the next service station was one hundred miles away. He bought a radiator hose and had it installed when Warren finally got back to me. If the man who helped us hadn't done so, it would have been a long time along side of the road. When Warren asked him how much we owed him, he said "Well my wife travels these roads and I just hope if something happens to her somebody will help her so I'm just paying my dues."

After this happened we stopped to help somebody else who had broken down on the road and a weasel went up the woman's dress. She started dancing and screaming and her husband and Warren whacked the animal and it finally ran off into the desert. She seemed to be ok. Later on we thought about how strange that was and hoped the animal was not rabid. I've never heard of anything like that ever happening before or since.

The Nav-Aid school was a tough one, especially for techs who had gotten their trade in technical school and were lacking a high school diploma or formal training in math. However, there was no choice, either get it or be down graded. The failure rate was something like 80%. We made the long drive to Oklahoma City from Pendleton in August and got the same parking place for our trailer that we had last time. It was fall though, and the swimming pool was empty. It wasn't quite the same group of people or the same camaraderie that we had enjoyed earlier. We always seemed to be happy wherever we were though, so all was okay. Gayleen started kindergarten there which she then had to start over in Pendleton when we had to return. Carl Rosati and his family had moved to Oklahoma City, where he was teaching at the Academy, which was a happy reunion and we got to get acquainted with his wife and children. Carl tried to help Warren, but it was too much and Warren flunked out at Thanksgiving time. Back then when you flunked you were sent home. That doesn't happen any more, now they try to help you succeed, but back then it was a real downer. This was happening to a lot of technicians. It was back to Pendleton for us. The trip was made with few incidents. We ran into some black ice in Wyoming. It took three hours to go ten miles and we stopped for a bit. I also ran off the road on a slick spot and a snow plow came along and pulled me back on the road. We didn't leave Oklahoma City until after Thanksgiving, even though that meant taking annual leave for the trip home, but it all worked out okay.

When we got back to Pendleton we got a space for our trailer up on the hill where the airport was located. It was a nice big park with big lots. There was a single row of about five trailers and that was all. The rest of the airport area was mostly old WWII barracks style structures, many of which had been made into single family dwellings and duplexes. We liked living up there.

Gayleen got started back to school. She took the bus, which she loved. She did very well in school in Pendleton. She was put into the "accelerated" first grade after a successful year in kindergarten. She loved school. There was a little store across the street from the school where the kids could take their pennies and buy candies, etc. When we were getting ready to leave Pendleton on the last day of school, Gayleen went to the store and bought me a malt ball and then forgot it at school. She was very upset about that and I've always remembered. When we left Pendleton for California it was during the Christmas vacation break in December, 1962.

During the summers of 1961 and 1962 I worked at the Weston Pea Cannery in Weston, which was about fifteen miles from Pendleton. I worked in the Personnel Department during the pea season, when they kept that office open around the clock. The first year I worked the graveyard shift, which was really tough but we didn't need any babysitters by my doing that. The following year I worked the swing shift, which was very busy and I liked it. We also didn't need any babysitters for that shift and I could get more sleep. It was fun but I was always glad when the season was over. It was here they were experimenting with a brand new process called "freeze-drying." It was all top secret, but those of us who worked there got to see some of what was going on. In order to properly "freeze dry" peas, each pea had to have a small puncture to let the moisture out. There were lots of jokes about the machine they were working on to provide these punctures, the "pea-pricker." It was also here that I saw a very black man with brilliant blue eyes. It was a mouth dropping open situation because it was so unexpected. It was also interesting to me that when they were running a line for frozen peas they frequently were packaging two brand names at the same time. Since there was often a price difference between these two specific brand names in the grocery stores, it was significant to me that the peas inside the packages came off exactly the same line.

There were two major historical events which took place while we were living "up on the hill" in Pendleton. One was John Glenn's flight into space, which took place on my birthday. The women were planning a surprise birthday get together for me and I was so excited about John Glenn that I didn't want to leave the radio. Finally the next door neighbor convinced me to come over to her house because she had a TV, so John Glenn and I celebrated that day together. I will always remember it. John Glenn didn't know a thing about my day.

The second event was the Cuban Missile Crisis. The FAA went to the next to the top alert status, which meant all leave was cancelled and every employee had to be within telephone contact at all times. It was pretty scary. We couldn't leave the house without telephoning in where we would be. As a result, we just didn't go anywhere for the two or three days all this took place. We also packed up a "survival kit" and found an old abandoned concrete culvert which went back underground about 20 feet, which was the best we could do to come up with some kind of protection for the family should it be needed. We hauled water and other necessities down there and stored, so if Warren was put on top alert I could get the kids and manage to take care of us. At top alert he would have to go to the airport and stay there. He would not be able to come home until the alert status went down again. No one else seemed to be doing any specific planning, but everyone was doing a lot of worrying. As everyone knows now, Khrushchev backed down and the crisis was over. It was a very tense time.

We got up to Royal City to see Edna and Irvin and kids about every other month. We had a lot of fun together and the kids enjoyed being on the farm. Edna's three youngest and our three were the same ages and sexes. John and Lester were just six weeks apart in age. Patty was born in April 1956 and Gayleen in August. Becky was born in October 1957 and Jan was born February 5, 1958. In 1960 there were four boys born in the family: in January Ivan Ellis Nanney III to Junior and Helen, their first boy and fourth child; in March our John Ellis, in April, Lester, Edna and Irvin's sixth child and fourth son and in June Jeffrey, Marge and Leroy's fourth boy. We shared maternity clothes.

1962 was also the year of the family's first divorce: Bob and Dorothy's. I guess it should not have been unexpected. Dorothy had wanted to become a nurse for years and Bob had fought her because, he didn't want his wife to work, and being a Christian Scientist, he didn't want her to be a nurse. The family finally convinced him to let her go to school, since that's what she wanted to do, but he just couldn't ever come to any reconciliation about the situation. The kids were pretty hurt by the situation and didn't get over it for many years. Dorothy quickly made a brief and disastrous second marriage and then a marriage which lasted until Loren Summer's death in 1990. She then made a fourth marriage with Ray Ogle which was brief, but happy, until his death.

The years were starting to go by and friends and family were beginning to go in different directions. It was just small dents happening at this time, but one could foresee that change was coming.

Leroy finished college and got his degree in Agricultural Engineering, the first of both his family and Marge's family to go to college. He went to work for the Soil Conservation Service in Idaho, but was already thinking about foreign service. Another ten years would pass before he and Marge packed up and moved to Lesotho, to Kenya, then to Zambia and finally back to Nairobi, Kenya. Marge became a Christian Science practitioner and lecturer and served on the Board of the Mother Church in Boston. We never were able to resume the close relationship we had before Warren's death. However, somehow we stayed in touch and I was called when Marge died on her birthday in 2008.

During these years, I visited my grandparents a couple of times a year, once by train and otherwise by driving. I always loved these visits and went to see them as much as I was able. Their health was beginning to deteriorate, however, and they died in 1966 and 1968 respectively. Daddy always chuckled, however, because when Grandpa died Grandma immediately had some repair work done on their living room. Years before, when they took out a partition between the living room and the dining room, Grandma was never happy with the ceiling. She always felt as though anyone coming in could see where the wall had been between the two rooms. She was very satisfied with the results of that repair. Both my grandparents died from lung cancer.

Warren was obliged to finish his Nav-Aids training by correspondence and it was a difficult situation for him. He did finally manage to complete it and received his GS-11 rating and certification for VOR, RCAG and ILS systems. He continued to go to short schools in specialized subjects and spent most of his free time on busman's holidays, building and tinkering with electronic gadgets. He also did all the repair and maintenance on our automobiles and appliances. In the years I was married to him we never had anyone repair or maintain anything. However, this did require the purchase of many specialized tools. I am sure money was saved over the years, but I'm not sure it was as much as might be imagined.

Pendleton was famous for two things: 1. The Pendleton Round-Up, rated in the top three rodeos of North America (the other two were Calgary and Cheyenne). 2. The Pendleton Woolen Mills. Living in Pendleton, one could go to the woolen mills and buy seconds, which were sold quite inexpensively. I wish now I would have really taken advantage of this, but at the same time, even though inexpensive, they seemed like something we could do without, so I never did buy anything. The Round-Up was something else. The whole town of Pendleton closed down (or opened up, as the case might be) for the Round-Up. The schools closed. It was a real civic affair. We always went both to the rodeo and to the Pageant which, even at this time, has some fame outside of Pendleton. Several Native American tribes, especially the local Nez Perce, were represented at the Round-Up and set up a whole tepee village, where they sold native made goods, danced, etc. It was like a big county fair to us, but it was a rodeo. I had grown up with rodeos. Sun Valley had a rodeo, as did both Nampa and Caldwell.

Pendleton was the first rodeo where there were different kinds of riding events from those I had seen before. Especially interesting was the wild horse riding. The only event I have never enjoyed or wanted to watch is the Brahma bull riding. I have seen too many people hurt by these bulls to get any pleasure out of it. I do like the events that depict actual activities cowboys on a working ranch have to do, such as steer wrestling or calf roping and I liked the wild horse riding because no spurs are needed or used.

My dad had been well known as a rodeo photographer as well as a snow photographer in his earlier days. From the time my parents moved to Nampa, he was the official photographer for the Snake River Stampede in Nampa, which was from 1951 through about 1975. In the 1950's he had the "National Rodeo Picture of the Year." Also during the 1950's he was gored in the knee by a bull. That must have been approximately 1955 because it was after Warren and I were married. This was the knee that eventually went bad and was replaced by a stainless steel one during the early years of joint replacement surgery. When he was hurt he was rushed to the hospital and when Elaine arrived breathlessly to see how Daddy was, he said "Did you get any pictures?" This was a typical comment from my dad, but was not accepted very well by Elaine. He was always on the lookout for the picture and never worried about what physical danger might result. Through Daddy's rodeo picture days he met a good many western "stars" such as the Sons of the Pioneers, who were famous for singing "Tumbling Tumbleweed," Roy Rogers, Gene Autry and others.

About this time, too, Daddy was very active in National Photographers of America. He and Elaine had started an Idaho chapter of National Photographers and served as President for quite a few years. Elaine was also active in this group. They made one trip to Europe with the Photographers and then made a teaching tour to Japan when Vicki was living in Korea. Daddy became a "master photographer" in commercial photography and Elaine won many awards for portrait photography. They were in demand as judges for various shows around the U.S.

Daddy made advertising motion pictures for Idaho Power, Morrison-Knudsen and Boise Cascade. I remember the first movie he made in the 1950's. Idaho Power was hesitant to let him do the finish editing. Daddy went to Denver for the editing and Idaho Power hired a union photographer from Hollywood to check Daddy's editing as they went along. The "professional" photographer said that Daddy's editing was as good as or better than anyone's. After that no one had any problem with Daddy doing all the finish editing on the films he made.

Another event I remember is one time when he was making that first Idaho Power film, Warren went with him to help with all the equipment. The filming took place in American Falls, Idaho, and Idaho Power opened up all the water so that the falls were full for the pictures. Warren helped with climbing up or lowering all the equipment Daddy wanted. Then Daddy would set everything up, and look and look through the view finder. Then he would say, "Nope, let's move right over there" pointing a few feet away. So they would pull everything back up or down where the whole operation was done over again. It usually took a dozen tries before Daddy was satisfied with the angle of the shots. That's the kind of photographer he was and his beautiful finished pictures, both still and movie, showed his perfectionism.

The pictures he made for Idaho Power when the Hell's Canyon Dam was built were always, in my opinion, works of art. I have never seen pictures of a construction site look so beautiful. He also took pictures for Morrison-Knudsen in 1948 when they were heavily involved in several large construction projects in Alaska. They would hire a small plane and Daddy would insist on taking the door off from the side where he would be taking pictures. He was absolutely fearless and had an innate admiration for the bush pilots of Alaska, who flew by the seat of their pants. He never tired of explaining to amazed people at home how the pilots in Alaska would check their air speed, look around at the country and then fly in a specific direction for a specific amount of time and then make a turn. They would then check their air speed again, look around and fly another direction for another specific time. All the time there are mountains on either side of them going up higher than they are flying. He was impressed and utterly fascinated. The bush pilots in Idaho were the same breed with the huge amount of "primitive area" in that state, where the only way in is to pack in or take an airplane.

Daddy and Elaine made several moves with their shop in Nampa. At first they lived on 7th Avenue South and their shop was on First Street downtown. They were only there for a year or so before they moved to 815 12th Avenue South, where they combined their shop and home at the same location. At that time they eliminated the retail sales of photographic equipment and went strictly to a studio only. They stayed and lived at this location until they retired. When they originally bought the shop from Braun Studios, a chain of photo studios in Idaho and Eastern Oregon, they had a ten year moratorium during which the chain would not come back to Nampa to compete with them. Braun respected that, but at the end of ten years they re-established their studio in Nampa. By the end of ten years my parents had established a very high end exclusive type of portrait and commercial photography business with a reputation to match. Their photography was expensive by both need and right.

The years in Pendleton were good ones and when they ended, it started a new era with us. For many years I called it the "end of the cowboy years" and the beginning of the "California years." We sold our plane while we were in Pendleton and started attending the Christian Science church. This widened the breech with my family, much to my distress. My grandparents continued to stay in close touch, but their health was deteriorating. Jack and Mid Eastep were our main friends in Pendleton and with their loss the only contact we had there was Howard Baker. This contact was broken with Warren's death. While we were in Pendleton we purchased a 10 x 50 three bedroom mobile home. This was five feet longer and two feet wider and seemed wonderfully bigger with 150 more square feet. We made the move from one to the other by pulling the trailers parallel with their doors opposite one another, placing lumber from one trailer door to the other, and moving everything straight across. This new trailer had what were called "Jack and Jill" bedrooms in the back, that is, two bedrooms across the back each five feet wide and probably seven or eight feet long. This gave the girls one bedroom with bunk beds and John the other with his crib. This was the trailer we moved to California. It was the only move we made with that trailer. It was becoming more difficult. Many states, California included, now required that only professional movers could move an oversized rig. With the extra width and length we were now over length and over width in every state.

We left Pendleton on January 3, 1963. The move south was uneventful compared with all our other moves. Later we figured that we had pulled our home 10,000 miles between 1958 and 1963.

Warren was scheduled to go to work at Moffett Field. This was near San Jose, where Alice and Babe lived, so we elected to go there, found a place to park the trailer temporarily and started looking for a trailer court to live in. We started near Moffett Field and worked our way south. We discovered it was no longer easy to find a place in a "mobile home park" as they were now known. Many parks had strict regulations about the size of trailers, awnings, screening around the bottom, parking of trucks or other vehicles, and lastly, but most importantly, children. We found that even though our trailer was quite new, we didn't have awnings; we didn't have screening around the bottom (although that could be remedied without a huge expense), our bread truck was not welcome and we had three children. Some parks had even started accepting only "double wides" which were becoming popular, but which we hadn't considered because they are impossible to move without a commercial hauler. In fact, when we reached the California border,

Vicki, Ellis, Doris, Elaine, Gayle

we determined that the regulations for pulling a trailer in California totally precluded us from doing it ourselves. We ended up hiring a commercial hauler to take us to San Jose. The problem with so many parks not accepting children was very bad. At one point in our search, our kids realized what the problem was and became very upset themselves. In any event, we finally found one park south of San Jose which was going to have a vacancy in their "families with children" section in about two weeks. We put money down on that spot and continued to stay with Babe and Alice while we waited. We finally got moved into our home towards the end of January.

Moffett Field was the first place Warren had ever worked where there were three shifts of electronic technicians working. He also was not completely happy there. There were a couple of the men he seemed to enjoy, but nothing like other places we had lived. We found that we were right across the fence in the trailer park from Roy and Eva Bailey. Warren had gone to Oregon Tech with Roy and so we renewed the friendship. We didn't have friends in San Jose with whom we played pinochle like we had in other places, but we enjoyed Roy and Eva, our own children were getting older and going to school and we were very involved by this time in church work.

Gayleen finished first grade at the school near the trailer park. One of her friends was a little girl named Rowena Provence and we got acquainted with Rowena's parents and little brother David who was the same age as John. We finally saw the handwriting on the wall as far as trailer living was concerned and bought a home through the FHA on San Pablo Avenue near Berryessa in San Jose. We still owned our home in Idaho. We sold the trailer on consignment through a trailer dealer and were able to get some money out of it in time to pay the closing costs on the house we were buying. The house deal closed before school was out, so Gayleen stayed with Roy and Eva for the last week of school and we got moved.

We loved our house in San Jose. It was a three bedroom, two bath, with a big fenced yard and about 1200 square feet of living space. That was really spacious after our years of trailer living. Gayleen started second grade at Toyon School within walking distance. We lived in this house at 14250 San Pablo Avenue from June, 1963, to October 1966, when we moved to Capitola. We became acquainted with our next door neighbors, the Gibsons. Our front lawns joined and Mr. Gibson always mowed the lawns "so they would look nice." We didn't have a lot of money to put into the house, but we did pour some concrete on one side and put in a small wading pool for the kids. Then we got suckered into an aluminum siding deal for the house. It was probably good in the long run, but did cost too much money. Part of the aluminum siding deal was the addition of awnings for our front windows. The house looked very nice when it was all finished. We had a water softener and one year Warren bought me a dishwasher, my first. Gayleen went through fourth grade at Toyon, Jan went through second and John went to kindergarten there. It was at Toyon School that Jan chipped her front tooth on the swings.

Dogs! Warren loved dogs and always had one, although they had to stay outside. We got Smokey, a mutt who looked like an Australian sheep dog, when we bought our house on Elm in Caldwell, Idaho. We had Smokey until our second trip to Oklahoma City from Pendleton, when Smokey was killed on the highway when he got loose one day. Then in Pendleton we bought a half Weimaraner, half Black Lab, we named Hambone. He really was a ham and loved to act up and make people laugh. We saw him actually climb the fence we had built to keep him in. He was a super dog and I really liked him. When we decided to move to California Warren way worried about taking an animal, because it's so much harder in the city to find a place that will allow pets. He found a home for Hambone with a man who had bought one of the other pups in the same litter and had become enamored of the combination breed, as we were. I am sure Hambone had a very good life and a very good home. After we moved to San Pablo in San Jose, we acquired Huckleberry, another black lab mix. Roy and Eva had just been given a little cocker spaniel mix they called Dusty. Roy was the one who suggested Huckleberry for a name. Roy had had a golden cocker spaniel purebred he called Sandy who had died a year or so before and somebody went out and got Dusty for them. It took Roy a while before he accepted Dusty because he missed Sandy so much. The two dogs were quite different. Anyway, at one time we had pictures of Dusty and Huckleberry together as little puppies. When Warren died I had Huckleberry, who was old and sick at the time, put to sleep. The only dog I had during my marriage to Warren was a little dachshund that I bought in Oklahoma City. I called her Cinnamon or Cindy for short. She was a warm wiggly lover, but Warren couldn't stand her. I found out later that dachshunds are notorious for running away from home and not being able to find their way back. When she ran away a second time, Warren refused to go out and look for her so I consoled myself with the idea that she undoubtedly found a home with people who loved her since she was purebred. It also seemed a good idea since I did not relish the thought of continuing disagreements over a dog. Most places we lived I ended up with a cat, but we never moved with a cat until San Jose. From that time all our cats moved with us when we moved. In fact, when we left San Jose, the cat climbed up on the roof and the last thing we had to do before we could completely vacate our house was to climb up on the roof and get the cat. I never got another dog until 2004 when I got my little shadow dog, Shadow. Shadow definitely lived up to his name, getting up to follow me when I moved across the room. When the girls left home Jan got a little mixed breed dog she called Himit and Gayleen got a dog she named Hilo. When Roy and I got married, he brought Dusty.

In 1963 I went to work for Valley Title Company in their typing pool. I was determined not to stay in the typing pool, so I worked very hard, didn't socialize much and concentrated on doing the best I could do. I was working at Valley Title when John Kennedy was assassinated. The company was owned by Congressman Don Edwards (D-Calif) and had many dedicated Democratic party members employed there. When word came of the President's assassination, Valley Title immediately closed its doors and everybody went home. It was grim. Of course, the President represents all of America, so even those of us who were Republicans and didn't like Kennedy's politics very well were overwhelmed by the thought of someone killing Kennedy. I know my thoughts at the time were that it was "right-wing radicals" like the John Birchers who hated Kennedy, who may have been to blame. Coming so soon after the Bay of Pigs and the Cuban Missile Crisis, one also wondered about Cuba's connection. The whole thing seemed incredible and impossible to have happened. I was also appalled at the thought of Lyndon Johnson becoming President. But, of course, President he did become and we all know now from hindsight the pathways and byways that history has taken, partially at least, because of this terrible crime. I don't remember how long we were off work, but the schools were closed too.

My children still remember watching the funeral on TV and how bad everyone felt. It was a terrible tragedy. The following year was an election year and Hubert Humphrey came to San Jose. Because of Valley Title's political connections, Mr. Humphrey came to Valley Title and shook everyone's hand, including mine. During those days after Kennedy's assassination, my thoughts frequently went to Franklin Roosevelt, who had died while in office. I was very young back then but I remembered how upset Americans were and how people were particularly upset with a change of President during World War II and the lack of confidence so many people had in Harry Truman's capabilities.

I made it out of the typing pool in three months. The opening was as an escrow secretary for Pat Hancock, a brother to one of the Vice-Presidents of the company and a very active Democrat. He had been a teacher who was caught up in the McCarthy era of anti-communism and Red baiting. He had been black listed for refusing to sign an affidavit swearing he was not a communist or did not belong to any communist organizations. He strongly believed this infringed on First Amendment guarantees and was illegal and unconstitutional. Eventually he was proven right. In the meantime, along with many others across the United States, he found himself out of a job. He was one of the first people to bring to my attention the long history of foreign intervention in Vietnam. The French were there for twenty years before leaving, allowing the United States to get involved. Pat was an anti-Vietnam War activist very early on. He was also active in the Don Edwards campaigns each two years. I got lots of information about politics while working for Pat. And it was certainly in contrast with the politics I learned from my grandfather.

In the meantime, I learned the title and escrow business and fell in love with it. After I left Valley Title, Pat told me he never found anybody else who could put out the quantity and quality of work that I did. We really enjoyed working together. His wife had some kind of mental health problems - I never did know exactly what. She ended up in an institution after several attempts at suicide. She seemed like a very nice person and Pat was genuinely in love with her. They did have a large number of children. After I left San Jose I lost touch with Pat and have always wondered about him and how his life went. He was a kind man and deserved some good fortune.

Irene came down to San Jose and spent six months living with us while she was recovering from being knocked down and gored by her ram from her flock of sheep. It took her quite a while to mend and we enjoyed having her with us during that time. She shared John's room with him. It also gave her an opportunity to visit with Aunt Marjorie and Alice and her family. In 1965, the family experienced a tragic and terrible accident that took three family members and severely injured two more. After Irene stayed with us for those six months, she went home for a few weeks and then decided to go visit Edna and Irvin for a while. She was there for a considerable length of time and decided she was ready to go home. Edna packed her mother and the three younger kids up and started out for the trip from Royal City to Homedale. We will, of course, never know exactly what happened. There was a place where the two-lane country highway crossed the railroad tracks. There had been at least one other accident at the same train crossing. Apparently the train hit their car directly and dragged it down the tracks until the engineer was able to stop the train. Edna, Irene and Lester were killed instantly. The girls, Becky and Patty were thrown from the car and found a considerable distance away. Patty, miraculously was not hurt but only received minor cuts and bruises. Becky had spinal cord injuries similar to the kind Aunt Marjorie had, but medicine had advanced sufficiently at that time so that she was eventually able to walk with half crutches.

I think it was Marge who kept trying to telephone us with the news, but I was working and she wasn't able to get in touch with us. Alice and Babe finally drove over to our house to be there when we got home. Of course, we dropped everything, packed up the kids and the car and the two families of us started the drive to Idaho. Our neighbors, the Gibsons gave us a hundred dollars, because by that time the banks were closed and we didn't want to wait until the next day to start the drive. We stayed with my folks for a few days but eventually went to Homedale, where all the family was gathered. We had Irene's funeral in Homedale and then drove up to Royal City for Edna and Lester's. The kids stayed in Idaho when we went up there, with my parents who were thrilled to be able to help. I found a thank-you letter for letting the children stay with them in my parents' memorabilia recently where they expressed appreciation for letting the children stay with them. It actually was the beginning of a better relationship for which I was very grateful. For some reason Marge and Warren were the ones who made all the arrangements and this put me on the periphery of all the planning. It was a noisy, chaotic and very difficult time. Most of the time I just followed along and tried to stay out of the way. The one thing I do remember is that all the neighbors of the Hardimans put up all of Edna's family who came. The house where we stayed only had twin beds and Warren and I ended up sleeping in one together, rather than sleeping separately. Everyone apparently had quite a laugh about that. We ended up staying in Idaho for a couple of weeks and then were able to go home.

Also while living in San Jose we made one vacation trip up the coast via Highway 1 all the way to Astoria, where we crossed the new bridge over the Columbia River. On the other side of the Columbia we turned east and drove to visit the Hardimans. There were no tourist facilities on the north side of the Columbia, so we ended up driving the whole distance because we couldn't find a motel. It was a gorgeous trip, however, and we always wanted to repeat it. The year must have been 1966. We made at least two trips to visit Irvin and family after the accident in 1965. With five children and a farm, Irvin had to hire a housekeeper. After several housekeepers came and went, Irvin married one of them and things settled down somewhat for him.

Unfortunately after going back to work at Valley Title Company I quit my job because I couldn't find a good babysitter. I had worked for about eighteen months until about the middle of 1965. In 1966 Warren quit the FAA and went to work "job shopping." Warren didn't really understand what "job shopping" was. It was a temporary work agency. He worked for IBM for several months and it came as quite a shock to him that when the job was finished, he went in to get his next assignment and was told that there was nothing available at the moment. He started looking for a full time regular job and continued job shopping until he went to work for Sylvania in Santa Cruz.

When we lived in San Jose we got very close to Aunt Marjorie McKiernon. We had visited her two or three times the year we lived in Needles and kept in touch by letter when we moved to Pendleton. When we moved to Capitola we were even closer and managed a visit in Carmel Valley almost monthly. Tom McKiernon and Warren got along famously, which was a blessing because Uncle Tom was somewhat of a loner and didn't get along well with many people. Warren would simply go out and involve himself in whatever Tom was doing. They both liked working with their hands and Warren could blend into Tom's activity without much problem. Tom built two sailboats during those years and Warren did his share of the work when we visited. They were beautiful boats and Tom had a right to be very proud of them. We went to Carmel Valley for the launching of the second boat. It was quite a huge affair. The side fence on their property had to be removed in order to get the boat onto the road. Then it had to be driven the 20 or so miles to Carmel and to a beach sandy enough to launch it. I suspect that because it was a catamaran a regular boat launch facility would not work for it. I was totally uneducated in anything having to do with nautical things. So was Warren. I might have a better idea of what was happening now, after thirty plus years owning a boat and living in Sitka, Alaska. However, it was a sail boat and that also is totally different. The boat was launched, the mast was stepped. It floated at the correct attitude and was perfection itself. Anything made by Tom would have had perfection as the only possible goal. The launching was an exciting day.

Aunt Marjorie over those years became the children's surrogate grandmother. She taught both girls how to knit, crochet, sew and do other crafts. She was so patient and loving and the kids loved going to visit with her. They always went one at a time so they would have Aunt Marjorie's entire attention. Every summer they went at least once to stay a week with Aunt Marjorie. Aunt Marjorie was very special to me. I always felt she was my mother substitute because I was able to talk to her about any subject in the world and there was unfailing courtesy and kindness. I will always miss her terribly. Tom was an alcoholic and Marjorie never talked about any of the incidents that occurred because of it. To her he was unfailingly courteous, strongly helpful and devoted. He took his marriage vows seriously. He was a man of contradiction but depth. Pattie had a very difficult life with him as he expected much more from her than was reasonable. She has never talked a great deal about it, but from what was said, it caused lifelong problems. For our family the time spent with them was precious and appreciated. I am very grateful for them being in our lives. Their part in my life was special and will never be forgotten.

I first learned about Aunt Marjorie shortly after Warren and I started dating. She and Tom had met in the army where both were serving in General Patton's army and fought up to where the Battle of the Bulge took place. She had been married to a doctor in Minneapolis, who was considerably older and with whom she had a "blue" baby who did not survive. Her married name was Thompson and she was known as Tommy to her many early and military friends. Her husband was also quite a well known and respected visual artist. We have a lovely picture painted by him, which Marjorie gave us. It is because of Aunt Marjorie and that part of the family that both Gayleen and Jan acquired the negative blood which they both have. We have determined that Warren must have had A negative blood since I have B positive and both girls have AB negative. Tom and Marjorie had gotten married and had adopted a little German girl, whose father was an unknown American GI. They had just been discharged and were planning a cross country trip to California to visit with family and to show Pattie, their new 6 year old daughter, the great United States. They met with a terrible accident crossing the bridge from New York into New Jersey, which totaled the car they were driving, put Pattie into a body length cast and made Aunt Marjorie a paraplegic. Warren and I had just married and I was recovering from polio when word of the accident reached us. I met Aunt Marjorie in the 1960's when we moved to California and we became fast friends and confidants which continued through my marriage to Roy and until her death in the 1980's. Roy and she became great friends and certainly she understood what his army life had been like and they shared many stories. She was, without any doubt, the most important role model of my life. I loved and respected her immensely. I continue to miss her and always will.

In the meantime, Babe and Alice left San Jose and bought some property at Moss Landing on Highway 1 between Watsonville and Monterey. Unfortunately, Warren was moving away from Alice because she had gotten involved in Rosicrucianism and Unity and he felt her beliefs were detrimental to our children. I had always liked Alice and felt uncomfortable with this, but I always went along with him at that time, so whatever he wanted did not receive any objection from me. We both joined the Christian Science church in San Jose. It was a pivotal move, especially for Warren. He had resisted joining for years, but finally decided it was what he really wanted to do. The biggest change was giving up alcohol entirely.

By 1966 Warren had become very unhappy working for the FAA at Moffett Field. That was sad because he had so totally enjoyed the work at Great Falls, Needles and Pendleton. Sylvania had opened a facility in Santa Cruz and when he had gone to them to see about a job, he was offered one immediately. He was very glad to leave "job shopping" and make a move to Santa Cruz County.

We moved to Capitola where we bought a house in Capitola and sold the San Jose house. The Capitola house was a beautiful house, in a lovely subdivision and we felt we had really moved up in the

The Hundred Year Stretch and Beyond

world. The house had a "family room" which we'd never had before and each of the kids had their own bedroom. The back yard was fenced. We planted some fruit trees and we were very comfortable in our beautiful home. We were excited about living on the coast and as it turned out, I never lived elsewhere other than on the coast again. We were teased by our San Jose friends about the fog and cold and rain that occurs near the ocean, but we were undaunted and soon learned that we loved that kind of climate. Roy helped us move and we rented a trailer and took many trailer loads over the mountain to our new house. It was about 2 a.m. on Halloween evening in 1966 when we finally completed the move. I can remember closing the garage door and the two of us stepped outside. Everything was so quiet in the neighborhood and we looked around and felt so good because it was such a nice neighborhood, the house was so nice and we were happy to be where we were. Shortly after we moved to Capitola Roy and Eva took a bid to Alaska and ended up doing relief work out of Juneau during 1967 and 1968. In 1969 they moved to Monterey/Salinas, California, where Roy worked until 1975. Roy worked the last six months of his 1966-67 tour in Southeast Alaska on Biorka Island.

Jane Provence and her husband had divorced and during these years Jane was living in Aptos, very close to Capitola. Warren worked evening shifts fairly often and when that happened Jane and I would take the children to the beach, where we cooked hot dogs and sang songs and enjoyed the ocean. The kids took to beach living like the water babies they were. John ended up repeating first grade and was still having trouble with reading so we got him a special reading tutor during that summer. The school officials wanted to label him "special education" and we wanted to avoid the labeling. The woman who tutored John, Miss Mary Jane Blood, had been a special reading teacher for years and she went to work with John. She felt that a summer of special reading classes would be sufficient to catch him up to his peers. By this time, we had made friends with Kay (Catherine) and Jim Hannibal. Kay became the kids' "second mother" and helped John with his reading that summer. He never had more than normal problems in school after that.

In 1969 Jane decided she needed to move to Casa Grande, Arizona, where her mother owned a home. Her father had died a few years previously and Jane's mother had moved to live with Jane in Aptos. It seemed financially more appropriate for them to move to Casa Grande than to maintain two homes, one in the more expensive beach area of California. So Warren and the kids helped move them to Arizona and get settled and then went on down to New Mexico to visit with Marge and Leroy, who were living there at that time. I couldn't get off work, so I stayed home.

Jane still lives in Arizona, although since her mother's death she has lived in Springerville. Her daughter, Rowena, still lives in Casa Grande.

Warren and I purchased five acres of country property near La Selva Beach in 1970 from George Liberty, who had ten acres and kept five adjacent acres for himself when he sold to us. It was a gorgeous piece of land with boysenberry and blackberry fields, zucchini and broccoli to the west, and open unused land on the other three sides of us. We were up on a hill with a three hundred sixty degree view. There were a few scattered houses and a lovely grove of live oaks. In exploring I found a wild forest garden of wild iris and other wild flowers on our property. It was a beautiful place with tremendous possibilities. Towards the end of 1969 I decided I wanted to go back to work. I went back to work for Title Insurance and Trust Company in their Watsonville office the first of January 1970. There had been some turnover in Watsonville when Bill Connell, who had worked for TI for many years in Watsonville, quit and joined First American, who promptly opened a Watsonville office and put Bill in as escrow officer. Naturally he was formidable competition. The third title company in Watsonville was Penniman Title, a privately owned company which had offices only in Santa Cruz County and had also been there for twenty years. The new escrow officer for TI in Watsonville was Jack Stone, a brash go-get'em, gung ho" type of guy who promptly set about shoring up TI's image and trying to keep as many customers as possible from switching to Bill's new First American office. I loved the title and escrow business, and was the happiest of my entire working years at TI. A year after I started work Jack had left his position and I was given his job and two secretaries. These were the years of the real estate boom in California and jobs in the title and escrow business were available. Monterey and Santa Cruz counties still had a great deal of open and agricultural land, which was being turned into subdivisions. I was very busy in the Watsonville office and was frequently the escrow officer for TI in Santa Cruz County with the most active real estate sales.

By that time John was almost eleven, Jan was thirteen and Gayleen was fourteen and they became latchkey kids, taking care of themselves until I got home.

By the middle of 1972, Sylvania had closed their Santa Cruz doors and Warren was working on his own as a freelance electronic technician. To be honest, I didn't pay a lot of attention to what he was doing. He brought home some dollars and we were totally engrossed in the improvements on our new property. I was working and made enough money to pay the bills and we were happy and very busy. The Libertys had given us one-half interest in their well and we ran the pipes up the hill from the well to the house. We had a large septic system installed. We had electricity installed from the Libertys to our house site. And we worked on floor plans. We finally settled on floor plans that we could afford, arranged financing and hired a contractor who agreed to allow Warren to do a lot of the work. He did all the electric and a lot of extra niceties like a system for voice and music to be played wherever desired. We also did the roofing, painting and varnishing, wall papering and finishing work.

We also got busy and sold the Idaho house, the San Jose house and the one in Capitola along with all the stock we had been given and used the money for the new house and for Warren's new business. I was working full time and working on the house evenings and weekends. The kids slept outside all summer and we slept in our little travel trailer. We moved into the big house as soon as it was livable and the Capitola house was sold. Things were tight financially, but we were getting by.

Working for Sylvania Warren had come up with several ideas about industrial controls. His business was centered around those as he worked to design controls specifically for manufacturing firms who had indicated an interest in more automatic processing. Warren worked long and hard on his industrial controls and had jobs with several companies, working on control systems within their operations. Part of the time he was working on systems already in place, repairing and maintaining them. Some of the people with whom he was making contact seemed interested in his ideas and were planning to let him make presentations when he was ready to do so. His idea involved making up a control system that could be modified for almost any kind of operation to automatically operate various controls needed by that specific industry. He did not really get far enough along to make it a viable concept that could be finished by someone else. The other problem as I can see it from the basis of many years down the road, is that computers were going to be coming along to do exactly the same operations he had in mind. His invention would have used relays and other mechanical devices, so I am afraid his work would have been outdated before it was finished due to the pace of advancement of computers. It was a wonderful dream that never came to be.

In the meantime, Gayleen was taken in by drugs and alcohol and no perception of life's goodness. She was obviously acutely unhappy, while acting as though everything was a big party just for her. Gayleen attended Soquel High during her freshman year and Aptos High during her sophomore year. She ran away from home for the first time in 1971. We were called by the juvenile authorities in San Jose, where she had been picked up and we drove over to pick her up. She had told them she was pregnant, which was not true. She then decided she did not want to live with us any more. If we would just let her go to Idaho and live with Gayle, that would be wonderful. Elaine thought that was a wonderful idea. Gayle and Phil agreed to take her and Warren agreed that it could be a good move. I resisted vehemently but eventually I acquiesced to the overwhelming majority and agreed to let her go. We lost Warren in the middle of that school year and I insisted that Gayleen finish her year in Wilder, which she did reluctantly.

Jan was always the good kid. We had no problems with her while growing up. She tells me now that was because she was always "able to get away with things" which Gayleen and John never could because they were not as careful, were more open and always got caught! I think about that statement on occasion.

Gayleen began to be our problem child. Hindsight is always so good. I can see the symptoms of bipolar disorder. She would always go into projects with grand ideas and high expectations and planning to conquer kingdoms. When she could not live up to her unrealistic goals, she would crash. In fifth grade, Mr. Westberg managed with her quite well, but dedicated and innovative teachers are not that common. We managed to get her interested in clarinet and competitive swimming, which she seemed to enjoy. She was minimally involved in 4H and church. She was possessive of friends and therefore kept few. She had temper tantrums and frequently provoked fights with Jan and John and learned how to get them to do her work for her. She was always sure no one really liked her. We tried in so many ways to make her feel like she was special allowing her to go with one or the other of us on trips, etc. We understood exactly what she was saying but were totally helpless to make her realize she was a very special and loved child, along with Jan and John. She was always positive that Jan was the favorite. I am sure this had an effect on Jan too, since she would have been aware that we were making special efforts to make Gayleen feel more loved even though they were futile.

Warren became ill during 1972 when Gayleen was in Idaho. As his health declined, he became convinced that he was going to die and he continuously told me he wanted to use Christian Science and under no circumstances did he want to go to a hospital. This conversation was repeated and I finally promised him I would abide by his decision. I had enough money to hire a Christian Science nurse, who worked full time with Warren for two weeks. At the end of that time I had to let her go because there was no money to pay for her services. Warren's sister Marjorie then came to California to stay with us and take care of Warren both physically and metaphysically since she had become a Christian Science practitioner. She was followed by Bob's second wife, Claudia, who was also a practicing Christian Scientist. They both stayed until Warren's death January 8, 1973. Acceding to Warren's wishes, we did not have a funeral. He was cremated and his ashes were scattered on the Pacific Ocean by plane. My parents came and stayed a few days. I went through the days doing all the practical and necessary things, got the children back to school, including Gayleen back to Idaho, putting the big house and property up for sale, since there would definitely not be funds to keep it, and finding and buying a smaller home in La Selva Beach. I couldn't seem to organize and figure out how to get us moved, so the church folks rallied and spent two days getting us packed up and moved. Amazingly, everything was packed, moved and unpacked, including furniture. This included potluck food for everyone who helped and for me and the children! I will forever be grateful to those good, kindly and thoughtful people who so lovingly cared for us in a time of emotional breakdown.

At the time of Warren's death, Bob came to see us. Junior didn't and regretted it forever, unfortunately. Alice came and Warren refused to see her, which broke my heart. I was never able to understand his feelings and reasons. However, Margie seemed to understand and she said she had talked to Alice and explained.

Gayleen had come home from Idaho for Christmas, then gone back to Idaho. When Warren died she came home again. She wanted to stay home, but I explained that it was her desire to go to Idaho and she had her father's blessing, but that I had never approved. Therefore, I felt it was important that she finish the year and then come home. I stressed that the purpose was simply to take a position about finishing what had been started to assert reliability. She reluctantly agreed and returned to Idaho to complete her junior year of high school in Wilder, Idaho. John went with her for a short visit. The stay in Idaho in the long run was not a good idea for many reasons and I was greatly relieved when the school year was over in May and she came home.

A couple of weeks after Warren's death I drove to San Francisco to pick up John and the drive home via Highway 1, which was the coastal route. It was a rainy, dark night on that two-lane rural highway. Just a couple of miles past Davenport an oncoming van with bald tires hydroplaned on a curve into our lane and we didn't see them at all until they slid sideways across the highway in front of us. I was driving a two-door Mustang, which was spun around in a circle as the van continued across and off my side of the highway. It didn't seem like any time passed at all before the police were present, wanting to get us out of our car. Apparently I was in shock, because I refused to get out of the car until "my babies were gotten out." Jan had been asleep in the back seat and John was seat belted in the front passenger seat. Jan told the officers that "my mother's babies were twelve and fourteen years old." Jan was able to squeeze out past me, got my purse out and gave the officer my driver's license and found the car registration. I had put a hole through my lip with my teeth and as head wounds are wont to do, had bled copiously, frightening John. He was crying, "Mom, please don't die." And I kept telling him I was fine. The one arriving ambulance took the occupants from the van directly to the hospital. The police wanted to get another ambulance, but for some reason I was adamantly opposed to going anywhere in an ambulance. A young man had stopped to help and offered to drive us to Santa Cruz to the hospital. The police asked to see his driver's license and he told them he didn't have one. They asked him why he had stopped. He said, "because there were people hurt and I had to help."

They let him drive us the remaining few miles to the hospital, where he promptly disappeared. Jan continued to take the adult role and called the Hannibal's, who immediately came down to the hospital where we were being examined and I was being sewed up. They took us to their home and we stayed with them that night until I was able to put myself together appropriately. John had no injuries except for bruises and some abrasions. Jan chipped her tail bone.

The following month I had a tooth abscess that needed either a root canal or to be extracted. I couldn't afford a root canal so had it extracted. One of my friends from the real estate community took me home from the dentist's office and made sure I took the pain pills and had a safe place to sleep for the rest of the day. She worked from home and was able to look in on me off and on for the rest of that day.

As I am recalling all of this forty plus years later, I am poignantly reminded of events immediately following Roy's death in 2011. The pain of losing someone special must cause our mental states to become less than stable, even though we may think we are doing just fine. Those around us can tell that we are not "doing just fine." I am even considering the possibility that I don't remember events properly. Jan and John have questioned my version of the car accident, not from the standpoint of the accident itself, but that it happened on the way back to Santa Cruz after delivering Gayleen to the airport to fly back to Idaho after Warren's death. After some time re-thinking the logistics, I concur that the following is the better scenario: John went to Idaho the first part of February after Warren's death, (it may have been spring break and it may have been later in the month) and returned a few days later. Jan and I were picking John up from the airport and driving home when it occurred. We all agree it was a dark and rainy night and that the three of us were in the car. Since my memory was obviously impaired after Warren's death, I have come to the conclusion that those small details are not really important. The accident occurred as described and I finally put myself back together again. We moved to La Selva Beach, where we lived until the move to Alaska a year and a half after Roy and I were married on December 14 of 1973.

I have frequently called 1973 my "lost year." I went through the motions of living but I can't remember much. I had a huge amount of guilt because I didn't provide the support my children should have had. The only thing that kept me going was my job, which I loved, and Roy's love, which I was earning. I was operating on automatic. I don't remember most of what I did, what transpired, when people came or left, whether meals were made or where everyone might have slept, how we got all the essentials accomplished, or how life continued. And at this point in my life, I am the only one living, other than my children, who might know at least some of it. Marge and Leroy came back with a U-Haul truck shortly before our move to La Selva was completed and I gave them a large number of tools and other things belonging to Warren. I also gave Marge our International truck, I was glad to have Warren's truck and the other things find a good home.

Shortly after Roy and I were married, he and I had a long talk about his niece whom he and Eve had living with them at the time of their divorce. He had wanted to adopt Anita. He asked me if I would consider it. Of course, I said yes. Anita was his sister, Carmen's, daughter. His sister had moved away shortly after her husband, David Howard, Jr., had died and nobody knew where she was. Anita had one sister and two brothers. Dee, her sister, lived in Baltimore and had lived there for a considerable time. The two brothers, John and David, as well as Anita had spent many years in and out of foster care. Neither of the boys wanted to live with Roy, possibly because of the reputation in the culture of the maternal uncle, who was supposed to take care of his sister's children and provide the discipline that parents were unable to give because of being so attached to their children. Anita and Roy seemed to be very bonded. Roy found out about Anita having married when he returned to California after our honeymoon. Anita called us several months later to say she was expecting a baby and hoped we could come help her when the baby was arriving.

We made plans to go to Minot, North Dakota, where Ray was stationed. Daniel Roy was born on January 31st, 1975. Eighteen months later Dennis Ray Wilkes was born on July 14, 1976 and we made the trip to Rapid City, South Dakota. We enjoyed meeting our new grandsons and had a good visit with them. Several years later they moved to Sitka where Anita still lives. Anita is a wonderful daughter and came and stayed with us and helped during Roy's final illness. I have enjoyed her immensely. The girls have known her and been friends since we moved in next door to them in the trailer park having sleep overs together along with other fun times. An interesting side note is that when Roy received his delayed birth certificate which he needed for the Indian Land Claims, it shows his name as Roy Daniel Bailey. All of his military records show Roy NMI Bailey. He had gone his whole life thinking he had no middle name.

I have only been back to what we call "our big house" twice since we left. Once was early on with the real estate folks, when the buyer wanted me to show him exactly where the right of way back to our house was located. The second visit was, many years later when Jan and I went to Salinas for Mellissa's wedding to Nate. We drove back to La Selva and without Jan I would never have found it, because all the roads had been changed and my sense of direction has never been the best, to say the least. The 360 degree view is no longer there, as trees and shrubbery have been planted and grown. It was good in that it was no longer our "dream home" and I was able to fully close that chapter of my life.

Roy and Eva came to visit when I finally had sufficient presence of mind to call them to tell them of Warren's death. Roy was devastated. He and Eva were ending their relationship so he was faced with that change in his life as well as losing Warren, one of his few special and chosen friends. He called me a time or two to talk. Then he came out to see me and we went out to dinner. Then he would go a couple of weeks before he would be in touch again. In June he called and then came to visit. He told me that he had moved out of his home with Eva and was sleeping on the couch at the house of his friend and co-worker, Marvin Wells. Marvin was also going through a difficult divorce and understood what Roy was going through. It seemed like a very slow and careful relationship was building between us and we were having difficulty accepting what was happening.

CHAPTER 11

My Fourth Life

On December 14, 1973, Roy and I were married at my home with the Congregational minister performing the ceremony. Bill and Lilly Kimball were there for Roy. Clara, my secretary at the Title Insurance escrow office, and Pattie McKiernon were there for me. We flew to Maui for a week and then the kids drove down to Los Angeles and met us and we went to Disneyland together with them for another week. We were deliriously happy and had a wonderful time. Upon returning home, I had a red phone installed with a separate line since Roy had to be available for his work and he didn't trust the kids to stay off the phone sufficiently. In addition, I had forgotten to make my house payment that month and was roundly teased when we got home!

When Gayleen came back to live at home again in the summer of 1973, after her dad's death but prior to my marriage to Roy, she enrolled at the "alternative" high school in Watsonville and finished high school from there. For graduation, Roy and I took her on vacation to Alaska in the summer of 1974. She ended up staying in Sitka, where she became heavily involved in drugs. She was okay for a while after we got her out of that situation, but when Roy and I moved to Alaska in the summer of 1975, she was proselytized by the Children of God. This was the era of cult indoctrination of impressionable teens. Obviously, teens with undiagnosed mental health problems were prime targets. Gayleen felt loved and that she belonged. They got her off drugs entirely, which was good. At that point, I stopped helping her in any way. I realized that any money I sent was taken by the cult. When she called me in tears, saying she had an impacted wisdom tooth, I got the name, address and phone number of the dentist. I checked him out to be sure it was really a dentist and then sent the money directly to him. Contact with her was intermittent and seldom. I have often thought that this ordeal caused so much pain and tears that I used up my life's quota.

Roy and I were in a lengthy roller-coaster ride in our many-sided relationship that became a true love affair. The biggest hurdle in the very beginning was Roy's relationship with my children. He had never had any children of his own. Mine were almost grown, and also had not much parenting during the year between Warren's death and our marriage. Essentially what worked was that Roy was there for them. He insisted that I do the decision making. I resented that in the beginning, but quickly realized that it was a good decision and I could do it. Warren had always been the decision maker. I had to learn how to be one. Much to my surprise, I could do it. Roy always backed me up and never once told me he didn't agree with me. Knowing him as well as I do now forty years later, I am sure he did disagree on occasion, but he never said a word. Being forced to be a parent was good for me. I stumbled along and I believe that in the long run I did a reasonably good job. Roy and I took Gayleen on an Alaska trip the summer after our marriage after she graduated from high school.

I was fascinated by this place that Roy called home. We spent several days each in Anchorage, Juneau and Sitka. Gayleen seemed to be very happy in Sitka and wanted to stay. I was nervous about it but realized she needed to start an adult life and reluctantly agreed. Jo and Ted Schenderline, Roy's friends, agreed to keep an eye out for her, and she and Roy's dad seemed to make an instant relationship. Unfortunately, she wasn't ready and became heavily involved with drugs, lost the job she had gotten, and ended up in the hospital from a fall down the stairs at Castle Hill while under the influence. I called the doctor, but he asked what Gayleen had told me. She hadn't told me anything and I wasn't aware yet of what was going on, so he was unable to inform me, since Gayleen was eighteen by this time. Within the next couple of weeks I figured it out and, with Christmas coming, had her come home.

The year and a half after we were married but before we moved to Alaska was fraught with Roy having to learn how to live with three kids, Jan deciding she wanted to get married at seventeen, Gayleen's falling into and out of a deep depression and Roy and I wondering how we were going to learn how to live with each other. It was somewhat frightening and filled with learning a whole new way of life with a new rhythm and meaning. We barged through it and by moving to Biorka Island with John in 1975, we managed to start putting our lives back together.

In the meantime, in a part of our year and a half of married life before the move to Alaska, Jan had started dating "the boy next door", and John was getting along in school but worried me because he was using marijuana heavily. Unbeknownst to me, Jan and Larry wanted to get married and when she asked me what I would say if she decided to get married, I told her she was too young and for starters, she needed to graduate from high school. Gayleen had graduated from the alternative high school and decided to go to college. Jan transferred to the alternative high school and was working on getting her high school diploma a year early. Of course, I found all this out after the fact. Two things happened at that point. Roy and I discussed a bid to Alaska that he wanted to make. I was struggling with the kids and although I loved my job, I was strongly of the opinion that I was short changing the kids and I wasn't sure about how to correct that situation. After a lot of soul searching we both decided there were a lot of reasons that a move to Alaska would be good for us and good for the family.

Jan graduated from high school a year early and I planned the "dream wedding" for Jan to occur just about ten days before our move would take place. We would be going to Biorka Island, where Roy had spent the last six months of his 1967-68 Alaska tour. Roy gamely tried not to pull his hair out as each member of the family seemed to have different ideas about when, where, and how this move was going to take place. Gayleen and Jan didn't want to go to Alaska. Jan, of course, would be staying as a newly married, very young bride. Gayleen was sure she wanted to go to college and that her housing was no problem since social security would send her money, due to her dad's death. John would definitely go with Roy and I. I wanted to go to Idaho for a family visit prior to leaving for Alaska. John wanted to stay in La Selva with Jan and Larry and meet me in Seattle on the way to Sitka. For years Roy loved to tell the story of doing the paperwork for the government move with each of us traveling in different directions and modes.

The other entertaining story concerned Jan's wedding. Jan wanted to wear my wedding dress, which then needed alterations. Larry's mother Lynn was an expert seamstress who located some matching satin and made the necessary alterations. Jan was beautiful in my dress and I was very flattered to have her want to use it. The humorous situation occurred when Roy walked her down the aisle and then stepped back directly on the train. She tried to move forward and was not able to release the dress from Roy's feet. She started to giggle and turned around pointing to his feet entrapping her movement. He immediately stepped off with an "Oops" and sprinkled laughter from everyone present. When Gayleen was married three years later in a wedding on Biorka Island, Roy was glad there was no train for him to have to look out for.

This was my first move where the movers came and packed everything up and when they left, the house was totally empty. John stayed in La Selva Beach and I went to Idaho. We met up in Seattle about a week later and we flew together to Sitka. Roy had hauled our boat with my cats to Prince Rupert two weeks before John and I left. Roy took the ferry to Sitka. From there he used our little boat to get out to Biorka. When John and I got to Sitka via Alaska Airlines, Roy met us and then brought us to Biorka on our boat. We soon realized that the little 22 foot boat we had bought shortly after we were married was not going to be big enough to face the Southeast Alaska Pacific Ocean, coming and going to Sitka. On the way out to Biorka it was foggy and drizzly, a climate I had never experienced. For years Roy laughed at me asking him "Are you sure you know where you're going?" He finally made some comment such as, "Well, if you don't trust me, I can turn back." I realized how bad I sounded and sat back to enjoy the balance of the trip out to the island that was to be our home for the next three plus years.

Biorka Island had the Federal Aviation Administration living quarters for four families plus the Coast Guard Loran station with eighteen to twenty mostly young Coast Guardsmen. It was an entitled remote station for the Coast Guard where the men were not allowed to have families living there. The "Coasties" were there for a one-year duty rotation. These young men became companions for John. The only other children on the island belonged to the FAA contingent, which consisted of Roy, John and I (1), Mike Matthews and his girlfriend (2), Mike Godsil and his wife (3), and Frank Price, his wife and two children, (4). For FAA folks there were two single family dwellings and a duplex (upstairs and downstairs). We were fortunate to get one of the single family dwellings. All the FAA buildings are now gone from Biorka, which went to remote maintenance in the 1980's. The Coast Guard left the island when the Loran being used there became obsolete, also in the 1980's. Biorka Island had only one telephone. That phone went directly to the Coast Guard Loran Station. The FAA had an extension in our recreational building. I received a phone call from Gayleen early in 1977. She wanted to come home for a "visit." She told me that it would be necessary for me to send her a round trip ticket so that the Children of God would be comfortable with her going. I told her "no problem." We had our own boat on Biorka, which we occasionally used to go back and forth to town. When she arrived in Sitka, we immediately came back to the island. We never discussed her leaving. She never brought up the subject either. Roy talked to the Coast Guard station commander and he simply stopped having any phone calls for Gayleen forwarded to our side of the island. Being on an island sixteen miles from land was a good deterrent. She told me later that neither Roy nor I ever said or did the things she had been told we would. She was able to enjoy the wilderness life available living on the island and she had John as a companion. It was the perfect location for recovery from the indoctrination she had received with the Children of God. They finally stopped calling and she was free of them. There was no TV, one radio station in Sitka, and our life consisted of picnics, boating, fishing, and exploring. Jan and her husband were living in Sitka by this time, having moved from California and had secured work with the fish processing firm, Sitka Sound Seafoods. Gayleen lived with us out on Biorka for six months and finally moved into Sitka.

In 1978, Gayleen married Steven Jacobs on Biorka Island under the huge Sitka Spruce tree on the lawn in front of the three houses and the recreational building. What a wedding! Steve's parents came, my parents came and took pictures, and the little planes flew back and forth with passengers, the cake, food, flowers, everything needed for a wedding! We had made friends with Eric "Swanie" Swanson, a "Coastie" from the Loran station, who remains a close friend to this day. Swanie catered all the food. Mike Matthews' girlfriend made all the floral arrangements. What an exciting week that became for the whole island. Everyone on the island, except those who had work shifts, came to the wedding. Steve had arranged with the local Catholic priest, Father Miller, to officiate. Roy escorted Gayleen from our house to the area we had designated for the ceremony. The sun cooperated and gave us sunshine and warmth. John, Jan and friends had a great time decorating Steve's little boat with "Just Married" signs and other such paraphernalia.

These were the years that Roy and I spent learning each other. It was not an easy education. We came from totally different backgrounds, cultures and experiences. Coupled with that were two people desperately in need of loving and being loved, both having lost mothers at an early age, of feeling out of step with the world and old enough to understand that melding two such different lives would take time and a great deal of work and determination. We had the determination and found that the process of the learning curve, although both painful and happy, was fulfilling.

Living on an island which, although "only" sixteen miles from a town, was remote from other inhabitants, and was an experience in and of itself. There was a large maintenance building which could be used for personal building projects for the residents, as well as maintenance for the housing and official equipment for the FAA. A "transient quarters" was a two bedroom house available for traveling workers. A recreational building with a pool table and a small kitchen was available for social life and an extension of the telephone system. We could phone our grocery and other supply orders into Sitka and they would be delivered weekly along with our mail by the FAA boat the Fedair. There was one radio station in Sitka which reached us on Biorka.

Our primary recreational time was focused on outdoor activities. The weather was cool and wet around the year, seldom exceeding 70 degrees F. high or 20 degrees F. low.

The rainfall was usually in excess of ninety inches per year. Obviously there was no need for any clothing to dress up or to sunbathe in. Roy took my watch and explained that I had no need for it. I discovered that I was tired and spent the first several months luxuriating in all the sleep I wanted.

John quickly fell into the rhythm of wilderness living and enjoyed the freedom of outdoor life once he understood the need for a "flight plan" for activities away from the house. We got him signed up for school via Alaska's excellent home schooling program. With many families living away from so-called civilization, home schooling was part of the normal Alaska living situation. We also signed up for remote services from the Alaska State Library and every few weeks we received a box of books chosen using an "interest list" we provided the library. After our first winter on Biorka, we traded our 22' boat for a 28' cabin cruiser with two engines. That gave us the ability to not only explore the country around Biorka, but also go in to Sitka for medical purposes and/or shopping, as well as fishing trips around Sitka Sound. Roy provided us with a permanent buoy in Symonds Bay in the line with all the other boats belonging to residents. We took the boat out of the water during the hardest part of the winter, however. The dominant weather came from the southeast and the fall and winter months were difficult when the wind switched to westerly or northerly as the water could easily become treacherous. Roy was quick and thorough, teaching us safety, both on water and land. John may not have been fascinated with math or history, but he seemed to grasp the importance of the outdoor lessons that Roy was teaching him.

The three plus years we spent on Biorka were among the most satisfying and pleasant of my entire life. In many ways I felt as though I had dropped back into the environment of my childhood in Idaho with picnics and camping, hunting and fishing being prominent activities of life. We loved our new boat, christened "Doris Marie," and spent hours aboard on day trips and regular weekend overnights. Roy had only known me in a California big city environment and gave me six months before he thought I would want to go back. Forty years later I am still here! Interestingly enough, I never caught a king (chinook) salmon while we lived on Biorka. That exciting event happened sometime after we had moved in to Sitka and occurred off Little Biorka during the annual Salmon Derby when I caught my biggest salmon, a forty-two pound king. However, we caught silvers (coho) and pinks (humpies) right from the start. We also caught the ubiquitous rock fish and lingcod, dug for clams, dived for abalone, picked berries, hiked, explored and spent many hours listening to the quiet in the cockpit of our boat as we were anchored up.

We took many trips over the years in our beloved boat: circumnavigation of islands Baranof, Kruzof, and Chichagof. We went to Juneau for their salmon derby in late summer and to Haines and Skagway to play tourist. We watched the eagles at hooligan (eulachon) time in Haines, and took the White Pass train from Skagway to the 1898-99 gold rush starting grounds. We explored Gustavus and Glacier Bay. The trip around Baranof Island was particularly scenic and wild. The east coast of Baranof is quite different from the west coast and we overnighted in many wild and beautiful coves along the way, seeing Port Alexander and Baranof Warm Springs, among many other places. Among the points we visited in northern southeast Alaska were Tenakee Springs, Angoon, Hoonah, Elfin Cove, Pelican, Gustavus, and Klukwan. The last was visited when we went to an Alaska Native Brotherhood Grand Camp in Haines where Mark Jacobs, Jr., Judson Brown and Roy Peratrovich took Roy and I to a Duklaweidi (Killer Whale) clan house in Klukwan and adopted me into that clan. I am continuously reminded of how humbled and honored I was at that ceremony.

Before Roy and I were married a friend of his called him to tell him that his parents, Charlie and Olinda, needed some help. Charlie was going down to Revard's Restaurant every day with a mason jar to get it filled with soup. That one jar of soup was what they were living on daily. So Roy jumped on a plane and came to Sitka to see what could be done. He discussed the issue with the man who was in charge of the Pioneer Home to see if they couldn't be moved there. They would get three meals a day, their laundry, beds and room cleaning would be done for them and if they got sick, they could receive medical care. The State of Alaska would accept a monthly fee based on their social security income. Roy was able to get them moved into the Home so they wouldn't have to be moved out of Sitka, where Charlie had lived all his life and Olinda had lived most of her life.

One of the things we were able to do was hire a helicopter to bring Charlie and Olinda out to Biorka for the day. That was truly a memorable few hours and they were so appreciative of being able to come, that it was heart warming. Olinda sang us some Tlingit songs and showed us how she would have been beating a drum when she sang. When we got involved in various cultural activities after we moved into town, Olinda's present to us of singing and drumming was appreciated even more. We took them all over the island. Charlie always spoke of Biorka as the island with the "sugar sand", referring to the beautiful white sand beach there. There are very few sand beaches in Southeast, so that was a defining description for Biorka. On another occasion we took Charlie (Olinda didn't want to come) on our boat for a tour in the closer protected waters of Sitka. He was thrilled to go to places that he remembered from his younger years. He told us all about picking berries and getting beach asparagus and other delicacies. Everything seemed to be changed for him, but still recognizable. It was wonderful to have had these few chances to be with him and to get to know him. He had bonded greatly with Gayleen and she had often gone to the Home and taken him out for a walk. I am glad we had a few opportunities to have special occasions with him, especially because of his untimely death.

When we moved to Biorka Island, one of the pluses was that Roy could see Charlie and Olinda more frequently than he had been able when he lived in the lower 48. We tried to go visit them whenever we went to Sitka. In February of 1978, Charlie was sent to the Public Health Hospital on Japonski Island for what was considered to be a minor ailment. The Public Health hospital had been created to cope with the tuberculosis epidemic which was rampant in the 30's and 40's, and had evolved into the medical care center for the Native (Indian) population. This was before the Native community in Southeast Alaska organized the Southeast Alaska Regional Health Consortium (SEARHC) and negotiated to take over the public health hospital to serve the Native population in southeast Alaska. Since the time SEARHC took over the hospital on Japonski Island, of course, it has greatly expanded and now owns clinics in most of the villages and towns of southeast Alaska.

Roy and I were invited to go to Mazatlan, Mexico, where my parents lived for three months every winter, to visit and enjoy the warmth and the beaches. Gayleen and Jan visited Charlie and Olinda frequently while we were on Biorka. They learned that Charlie had gone to the hospital and so they went over to see him, but they discovered that he had unexpectedly died. We had not left an address or phone number where we could be reached, they called Aunt Dot in Blackfoot. Aunt Dot managed to go through the police department in Nampa to get the name of one of my parents' employees, and was able to get a phone number to get hold of us. When we got the notification of a phone call, Roy took off for the lobby to get the call. Of course, Roy was devastated. We got our plane tickets changed to a direct flight home from Los Angeles and were on the plane within a few hours. It was very sad because Roy had been looking forward to living in Sitka where, for the first time in many years, he would be able to see his parents on a regular and frequent basis. Olinda was distraught and no matter how anyone talked to her, she decided she wanted to die too. She refused to eat or drink or partake of life from the time Charlie died until she, too, died in the middle of May. Roy had promised her that he would take care of her needs and that she would get a "Christian burial." She had given him $800 to accomplish these ends. She trusted Roy and he was always there for her. He got in touch with Ronald Search, his step-brother, and arranged a flight down from Anchorage where he lived and gave him money for a hotel and meals, so that he could be there for his mother's funeral. Ronald was always appreciative of Roy's help. After all of Olinda's funeral expenses were paid the small amount of money left was given to Ronald. His widow let Roy know when Ronald died a few years later. She also gave him Ronald's watch. When we finally got orders to move into Sitka in September, one of the bittersweet parts of that move was the fact that we finally would have been able to be a more present part of Charlie's life and it was too late.

Our boating life was paramount in those years and we reveled in the wilderness and solitude and quiet of the rain forest, ocean and mountains around us. Our boating trips lasted anywhere from one overnight to two weeks in length. The longest trip, two weeks in length, was taken in 1980,: Sitka to Juneau (actually Auk Bay at the harbor) for a couple of days, stopping in Tenakee Springs for a few hours, then on to Skagway, where we stayed three or four days, then started back south down Lynn Canal, when a strong northerly wind came up, causing all the boats to scurry for safe anchorage. We got to Sullivan Island in the south part of Lynn Canal and got into a very sheltered bay, where we anchored and were in completely calm waters. It was sunny and warm and beautiful! We heated up some water for some lovely sponge baths and had a perfectly glorious few hours, enjoying being clean and in a totally private and beautiful environment! We were completely protected from the wild north wind blowing down through Lynn Canal! We ended up staying overnight in that spot. From there we went into Icy Strait and found an anchorage near the National Park lodge, and secured two sets of tickets for sight seeing in Glacier Bay National Park. There are two long fjords in the park and each set of tickets was for a trip up one of the two. The longest fjord was an overnight trip and the second set of tickets was for a day trip up the other. There was still a lot of ice in the Park then, so it was definitely a spectacular two trips. It was breathtaking and we took hundreds of pictures. I was spellbound with the scenery.

From Glacier Bay we boated over to Hoonah. We never actually got into Hoonah and we should have gone back, but never have been able to do that, unfortunately. We made our way home from there.

We moved into Sitka in late fall of 1978 and came back to the realities of community living. We bought a house there and continue to live in it to this day. John had completed his high school studies on Biorka via Alaska's home school program. He lived a few months with us but soon wanted to see the world. After talking to Roy at some length about opportunities available to him he ended up flying up to Anchorage to join the Marines. They didn't tell me until it was a done deal!

A few months after John had joined the Marines he finished boot camp and had come home for a visit. He told us about a wonderful girl he had met who was also a Marine and he had decided he wanted to marry her. He ended up being scheduled for

Okinawa and in order to be able to take a wife there he needed to get married, so all of us made plans to go to the Los Angeles area for the wedding. Steve and Gayleen, Jan and Aaron, Roy and I all went. Roy and I hosted the rehearsal dinner at a motel. Jeannette was a lovely young woman. Her father had been a Marine and had married her mother, a Japanese woman, when he was stationed in Occupied Japan after WWII. John and Jeannette were married at the court house in 29 Palms in order to make the deadline required for John to take Jeannette to Okinawa. Then they had the big wedding afterwards. Jeannette had a big family, 3 brothers and 2 sisters, and they adored their mother. It was a fun wedding. We thoroughly enjoyed meeting John's new family and our new daughter-in-law.

They continue to relish their marriage and we've often congratulated them on their excellent relationship. We enjoy Jeannette's family very much and are so glad for John that he has a wonderful family for support. We grieved with them when they lost their dad not long after John joined the family.

Biorka Island continued to be our favorite fishing grounds for the rest of our boating life. My dad came up to go fishing with us every year until we were forced to move to Santa Barbara to finish Roy's civil service requirement of length of service needed for retirement. Two of those years Vicki came with him. As he aged, his mobility diminished sufficiently for it to be prudent for someone to travel with him. Vicki and I bought a comfortable lawn chair to be set up in the cockpit for him to sit on while in the boat. He didn't like to put his fishing rod into the rod holders, but preferred to hold it. He loved just sitting and enjoying the feel of the rod and the beauty of the wild around us. He was always happy fishing. Roy always netted the fish as well as baited all the hooks. There were times when we had four rods out and if we got into silvers, it was mass chaos. The joy and excitement of those wonderful days remains with me always. The story I've always loved to tell was fishing with Daddy and Vicki up in Kakul Narrows where the channel goes from Salisbury Sound to Peril Strait. It was a gorgeous sunny day and we got into a huge school of coho (silvers). We started getting strike after strike. In the beginning we were just fishing with two rods out although there were four of us aboard. We traded around occasionally. Roy and I usually let Vicki and Daddy catch the fish because we got to fish all summer and they didn't. After Vicki had caught five or six silvers and then got another strike, she turned to me and said "Oh my goodness, another! I'm tired. You take the rod Dorie." I never turned down a chance to pull a fish on board so I grabbed the rod and started playing the fish. When we got it aboard, it turned out to be the biggest silver caught that day. I am guessing that fish weighed ten to twelve pounds or so. A fabulous catch of the day! A small commercial fishing boat had pulled up and idled beside the pattern we were traversing while we were catching fish after fish and we had a pleasant across-the-water exchange of words about our fishing luck. And a quick explanation of "pattern being traversed"...... The current is very fast in Kakul, perhaps eight or nine knots, almost as fast as Sergius Narrows so essentially Roy put the boat into forward gear just fast enough to keep us stationary while we were trolling. Roy always told the story of Charlie, his father, missing the tide through Kakul and spending three or four hours not moving forward but with the engine running in order to keep his boat safe in that current. Several times going through Kakul and then Sergius, the Coast Guard buoys marking the channel were lying over horizontal to the water at high tide. We had a very fast boat so we could navigate that fast current, although Roy, being as safety conscious as he was, did not like to scoot through Kakul and Sergius at high tide. Our kids, guests and their friends always wanted to do it.

One of our favorite anchorages was Poison Cove, which is located on up Peril Strait toward Hoonah Sound and Chatham Strait. This cove contained a place for a log raft to be tied off during the era of logging for the pulp mill in Sitka. It was easier to tie up to a log raft than to anchor, and safer, since we wouldn't drift if the anchor hadn't been set sufficiently. We loved the location and spent many hours enjoying our favorite locations. We definitely had "many" anchorages that we used and several that we were forced to use because of worsening weather during the Labor Day weekend which was the calendar marker between the frequently nasty autumn weather and winter to-be avoided weather. As the price of gasoline continued to go up, we stopped going up to Kalinan Bay and Peril Strait for a weekend and stayed closer to Sitka, heading out to Biorka or over to Goddard Hot Springs and Dorothy Narrows south to Whale Bay for our fishing and enjoyment. In Sitka, occasionally early in the fall and spring we would take a lunch break in our boat, heading out toward Silver Bay and anchoring for a quiet and quick lunch. We definitely loved this boating life and the very lucky ability to indulge in it.

When we moved into Sitka from Biorka, the moving company in Sitka used one of the owners' personal vessels to pack and bring all our belongings into town. It was quite a sight seeing that large pleasure boat loaded down with our personal belongings headed out of Symonds Bay toward Sitka. We managed to find a temporary rental for the three months it took us to find a house to buy and to move into it. Rentals were very hard to find in those days and there were few houses for sale. If I remember correctly, there were three houses for sale in our price range, one that was too expensive and on a very steep driveway, one that was definitely a "fixer-upper" and the one we bought! I had made a very expensive mistake by not buying a house immediately upon our transfer to Biorka. The house I sold in La Selva Beach had brought in enough money to put in a savings account to be used when we got moved. In the meantime, there was rampant inflation and houses were way more expensive than they had been in 1975 when we moved up from the lower 48. The three plus years we hadn't owned a car or a house caused some distress financially, which had never crossed my mind as a possibility at the time. We lived through it, of course, and I was wiser and more knowledgeable than I had been.

I found a job almost immediately after we moved into town. We had gotten a berth in Crescent Harbor for the Doris Marie and Roy enjoyed telling us stories and showing us around Sitka. We found out that there were lots of organized activities and the outdoor activities were boundless, especially with our boat. Sitka had consolidated their city and borough in 1971, so it was a municipality that had just one political body, the Assembly. Noontime brought Problem Corner, a radio show where people could phone in with whatever they had to sell or wanted to buy. They could also complain about pot holes or store hours. They could complain about local, state or national political issues or even the ever changing weather and the recent Assembly meeting. Almost all comments were civil and polite, although frequently heated. Alaskans have strong views. Everyone tuned in to hear Paul Harvey's news and his Rest of the Story and Problem Corner and went to all the school and civic activities. I suspect using the word everyone was probably not very far being totally correct. Local Assembly meetings were usually well attended. The Assembly was the elected group that legislated the laws for the city and borough, which included almost all of Baranof Island. Although the borough is large, its population is close to 99% citizens of Sitka. Even Baranof Warm Springs, with its dozen or so summer residents, seldom has any residents during the winter. There are a handful of residents living on seaward islands west of Sitka. Port Alexander on the tip of the island had opted out of the borough but it included the rest of Baranof and about half of Chichagof plus the small seaward islands and Kruzof, the larger island with Mt. Edgecumbe on it. The city and borough had an administrator/city manager who was the full time person in charge. The Assembly was headed by an elected mayor who was the assembly person who ran the meetings and was the face of the city at all the functions needing to be greeted and visited. Alaska's boroughs are similar to counties. However, the state's operations and elected legislature are very distinct. Just as an example, the state does not levy any taxes. Taxes, such as sales taxes are levied by municipalities. Property taxes are also levied by cities and boroughs. Therefore, there is lots of unorganized land which is not included in any city or borough and, therefore, there are no taxes. Of course, that means there are no services for those areas too. There are also several kinds of municipalities: Home Rule, first class and second class, plus unorganized and former. Sitka is a Home Rule municipality. Each has its own requirements by law. It is a very interesting and different way of government that I don't believe exists in any other of the fifty states. We had found a welcoming and comfortable home!

In 1982 we were faced with a very difficult situation. Due to political closed-door machinations, we were required to return to California which the Federal Aviation Administration deemed Roy's home region, to finish out his remaining three years needed to receive a civil service pension. We talked about three days about our options and painfully decided that the actions needed to protest were too emotional and would require confrontation we neither one could imagine being able to accomplish. So we packed up what would be needed for three years, put everything else in one of our bedrooms with a lock on the door, rented out our house, found a location for our boat and left via ferry in March for Santa Barbara, California, to finish Roy's required thirty years to retirement. The date that he was eligible to retire was October 25, 1985. His co-workers, at the beginning of October, 1985, made a count down calendar, which they duly marked off. We left Santa Barbara on October 27, 1985, bound back to our beloved Sitka.

We consciously promised ourselves that we would be happy with our three years in Santa Barbara and enjoy the many things that were good and pleasant about that lovely city. We loved the beaches and the sunshine, being able to make long road trips, the shopping and restaurants, bicycling, and being able to see our son and his family, who lived in the San Diego area. It was also easier to go to visit in Idaho or to Carmel Valley to visit Aunt Marjorie or to see some of the spectacular sights that the lower 48 has available. And we knew we would be going home to our rain-drenched island, our boat, our mountains and the wonderful community spirit of Sitka. I found a job with Santa Barbara Savings and Loan, managing their payment processing department and began my love of computers.

We did have many good times along with life's always present sad times, those three years. John's son, Warren, was born in March of 1985, Jan and her family came to visit us once, Gayleen came down when I had to have surgery, we had many good visits with John, Jeannette and their children, we watched a total lunar eclipse from the hills, we watched the Queen of England race by on the freeway when she visited President Reagan on his ranch, and had to move to a new apartment when all the rents were raised in Goleta because of the 1984 Olympics. We completely enjoyed the Greek Festival every year and the free music concerts on the grounds of the city government, which were held at the same time as the Santa Barbara Mexican Festival. Planning the move back to Sitka was an experience in itself. This trip would not be paid by the government, but was one we had to do ourselves. We ended up renting a U-Haul truck, which John agreed to drive from Santa Barbara to Seattle. After lots of pricing calls we found that Sampson Tug and Barge would set a container in their lot for us to use. We had to transfer all our furniture and boxes, which we had packed ourselves, to this container and place our own padlock on it. They barged it, along with a load of many containers, of course, and got it to Sitka (on their own schedule) where we had to go to their landing, where they set our container out so we could unload it ourselves. We had a three-vehicle convoy from Santa Barbara to Seattle - the U-Haul driven by John, our car driven by me and our little pickup driven by Roy! I kept remembering the convoy headed to Pendleton from Needles with three vehicles plus our airplane! We turned in the U-Haul in Seattle, sent John home via air and took our vehicles and ourselves to the ferry terminal, which was still in Seattle at that time. On the trip north to Seattle, if I remember correctly, we spent one night sleeping in our vehicles in a parking lot and one night in a motel. I may be driven by wishful remembering, but I believe we managed the whole move for about $3,000. Then our son-in-law and our dear friend Eric Swanson used his pickup to make several trips moving everything to the house.

Dear Jan had spent a week cleaning our house after our renters left, which was a very sad experience, and we got home to an empty oil tank, which had been full when we left to heat the house, along with a disaster so far as having a clean-and-ready-to-live-in home. But it was so wonderful to be home! We had done it!

We had a lot to do to take up our life where we had left it three plus years before. New engines were waiting to be installed in our boat and that project was first on our list. Then we had two remodeling projects on our house: remodeling the kitchen, which was the 1960's original and replacing the roof. The first was accomplished in the summer of 1987 with Roy and Ron James completely replacing all the wiring and the second in the summer of 1988.

The Alaska Native Brotherhood had its 75th anniversary in 1987 and Roy and I were elected as Presidents of the Brotherhood and the Sisterhood. That was a tremendous honor, but also a huge amount of work. We were enthusiastic and happy about it though, so we enjoyed all the work! Roy went on as President of the ANB for several years and was always active and busy in other years when someone else was President. He also continued with Tlingit and Haida Central Council, which he had begun while we were still in California. A childhood friend, Al Perkins, got him interested in tribal politics and he served several terms on the Tribal Council. It was these few years when I realized how much Roy enjoyed being a part of the social fiber of Sitka. I had always thought of him as a quiet, intellectual introvert. He was never so happy as all the years he spent involved with several Native organizations, as well as his years on the Sitka School Board. He had always teased me about "social mingling" when we went to an event sponsored by the City and Borough or by the Chamber of Commerce or the school district. I enjoyed all the social activities, but not to the extent Roy did. I much preferred social activities with just a very few people.

In discussing Roy's civic activities I am reminded that I should include my own. I am somewhat reticent talking about my activities, but one of the purposes of this writing is to inform my family about my life with the thought that it is a good historical thing to do and I've always been in favor of viewing history through as clear a lens as possible. There are so many things that I don't know about my own family and wish I had asked hundreds more questions than I did, since I grew up with the idea that asking personal questions was not polite and, therefore, not to be done. There is some merit to keeping the personal lives of your family private but there are also reasons to give your children information which may help their knowledge of themselves. It also is good for one's esteem to know of family traits which have been beneficial in making a person who he is. We smile over traits exhibited by family members which recognize the kind of people are in our family. When someone remarked to my dad, here for his annual fishing trip with Roy, that I was well known for my stubbornness, he said "she comes by it naturally." He was a constant thorn in Elaine's side, well known for his stubbornness. My only warning might be "Be sure you have examined the issue over which you refuse to budge with careful and thoughtful ways. There are times when changing one's mind is a good idea, whether for philosophical or political reasons of good standing."

Roy and I had been traveling and upon returning had stopped in at city hall to see what was happening while we were gone. I was immediately stopped and asked to pick up a candidate's package and run for assembly. That day was the last day to submit an application for your candidacy. It was something I had never considered, even in the nine years I had spent on the planning commission.

The urging of several people as I continued on my rounds of the city offices to chat, continued to pursue me. I finally went to the Clerk's office and got a packet. It was easy enough to fill out, but I needed signatures of twenty-five people registered to vote in Sitka. Someone grabbed the page and return it to me in a few minutes with several signatures. So Roy said "Let's go get the rest." So I ended up running for an assembly seat unexpectedly. I also learned that campaigning was not one of my favorite activities. I ended up serving two full terms. I enjoyed serving immensely and felt I was successful. It was extremely good for me. The biggest lesson I learned was how to handle conflict. I quickly learned that sticking your head in the sand was not a viable option. You must face the conflict and take a firm position. I lost friends, I gained friends, I changed my mind, I learned that compromise was sometimes impossible, but I continued to hold my head up high and continued to work for what, in my opinion, was best for the most. I was satisfied, for the most part, with the successes and happy about the learning curve I had climbed. I no longer have an avid interest in the debate on the issues. I am still uncomfortable with the depths of disagreement on some issues. My discomfort lies in the number of solutions that could be possible. I am very comfortable with being out of the decision making. It is extremely interesting to me that almost any decision made can be workable to fit the need. I was also very grateful that people of Sitka elected me twice to work for them.

Roy also left the political world, probably for many similar reasons. He seldom discussed his reasoning with me and I seldom discussed mine with him. Both of us were happy with departing the political world.

Getting our boat re-powered and ready to use was our number one priority. We had bought new engines while we were in Santa Barbara while we were still employed and had the money. We made a deal with the boat shop to install the engines and get the boat seaworthy. Roy had taken his retirement in the fall, so we had several months available to have this work done. We had been home in Sitka for almost ten years when we departed the political scene. Trying to put things in chronological order, we got home at the end of October 1985. Roy worked from 1986 to 2000 for SEARHC. He was very unhappy there, so when that job ended it was with both of our relief and approval. I ran for assembly in 2000 and again in 2003 winning both times. In 1987 we re-roofed the house and remodeled the kitchen area, putting all new electrical in and new appliances. We also re-wired the bedrooms and front bathroom. Then in 2001 we re-financed the house and put in the new master bedroom, which also included a new hot water system and furnace for the existing hot water heating. The new furnace meant we no longer had to bleed the lines, because the furnace did that automatically. We were still sleeping in our bed in the living room when the attack of 9/11 occurred. Roy came in and woke me up to tell me a plane had flown into one of the twin towers in New York City and nobody knew what was going on. I got up to watch TV and saw all chaos all the chaos and guesswork news reporting that was happening that day. It was very scary. I was worried about Gayleen and her family and John and his family. Every bit of news going out was suspect and it was difficult and essentially impossible to read between any lines. There was speculation said that a 747 had crashed in Pennsylvania that may have been headed to the Pentagon and then Roy and I speculated that we were under attack in some way. We felt reasonably safe here in Alaska, but were worried about John and his family in Southern California and Gayleen in Ireland. All airplanes in the air were directed to land at the nearest airport and were grounded until further notice. Amazingly the air traffic control people were able to get thousands of planes on the ground within a spectacularly short time. Fifteen years later we are still hearing the many stories. New York's fire departments and police departments did exemplary work. Thinking about the whole situation still brings tears to my eyes. I understand the chaos and tears much better now when I think about Pearl Harbor. I understand the terror and the total incomprehension of what's happening. How human beings can be part of destruction and wanton killing on this level is beyond my understanding. It was many days before any "real" information as to what had happened was available. I cannot fathom the agony of those who had family and friends lost in this catastrophe.

Roy had suggested to me a couple of months before this happened that he wanted me to take Jan to Ireland for a visit after her divorce from Bill Larson. She and I had talked about it and chosen a date in October, and I had bought the tickets. She phoned me on September 12th and said, "Well, do you still want to go to Ireland?" I said, "of course! Life does go on." We had a wonderful trip and I'm so glad we went. While we were there we took the ferry from Dublin over to Wales and drove to Llanfrachreth to the Nannau manor where the Nanney family came from when they arrived in New England and the "new world." There are no Nanney's left in England or Wales but there are lots of them stemming from that manor scattered all over what is now the USA. We did some research on the family while we were there and got some copies of stories and documents in historical files in Wales. We stayed at a lovely B&B and had arranged for a lovely dinner before we left to head back to Dublin. The people who owned the B&B were thrilled to have some Nanney's visiting.

We finished our wonderful visit to Ireland and returned to Sitka where we totally enjoyed our boat and did lots of both long and short trips on it, savoring the beautiful rain forest in which we live. We saw many of the animals who live in the ocean as well as those who lived on the land. There was always something new. We saw so many bays and fjords and islands along with snow-covered mountain peaks and waterfalls. We discovered that the east side of Baranof Island on which Sitka is located, is very different from the western side where we lived. We knew that Port Alexander, on the southern tip of the island, was a little fishing community. It was fun on one of our first lengthy boat excursions to leave Sitka, and travel down past Goddard and through Dorothy Narrows and then follow the coast line until we made the turn at Cape Decision to go north up Chatham Strait. It had been many years since Roy had been in these waters so he was extra watchful, as usual, as to where we were going. Seeing the terrain on the east side of Baranof was definitely an adventure. The mountains were steeper on the east side and the bays and fjords cut into the island at a steeper angle. There were waterfalls everywhere. It was beautiful. We traveled north to Baranof Warm Springs, where we stopped for a few hours to explore and take a hot springs bath, which was lots of fun. Then we continued onward up Chatham to Tenakee Springs on Chichagof Island, where I discovered thimbleberries and discovered they were the best- tasting berries among the many wild edible berries growing in the rain forest. I've looked for them near Sitka, but have never found any. There were lots of tasty low bush cranberries on Biorka Island when we lived out there but you needed to wait until after the first heavy frost to pick them so they would have the sweetest taste. I've usually found them on open muskeg where they get the most of the summer sun without shade. I learned that you needed to dress appropriately if you went after the low bush cranberries because you usually stepped into a muskeg hole and went in at least to your knees, so you needed to be prepared. On Biorka I usually came home muddy and wet, but the berries were really good and worth the difficulties in getting them.

From Tenakee we went on up to Auk Bay, where we felt like we were back in a city but were able to stock up on supplies and gasoline. From Auk Bay and Juneau we went up to Skagway. We didn't cross to Haines but went straight to Skagway and were able to dock and tie up in their boat harbor for the couple of days we spent there. We took the scenic tour on the White Pass train up to where the people on the Gold Rush built rafts to take them to Dawson and certain riches, at least they were sure they were headed to certain riches. It was very interesting as you could see part of the trail the Gold Rushers used to pack all the supplies required by Canada. The Canadians did not intend to have to take care of hundreds of men and women who had come, intending to go home rich and not realizing that very few even came close. Many of those who were headed to the Klondike hired Native men to help carry all the boxes of food and supplies up the mountain to get to where they built their raft to use to get to the gold fields.

Every person traveling to the goldfields of the Yukon Territory were required to take along one year's worth of supplies. Every dealer of goods was ready to tell them exactly what they needed, and would sell the products to them at a very high price. There were also many how-to books for the prospector. Many were written by people who were never in the wilderness, let alone the Yukon.

Railroad List of items needed by miners distributed by the Northern Pacific:

For each man:

FOOD:		CLOTHING:		EQUIPMENT:
200	pounds of bacon	1	suit oil clothing	1	large bucket
400	pounds of flour	3	pairs snag-proof rubber boots	1	set granite buckets
85	pounds assorted dried fruit	3	pairs heavy shoes	2	axes, plus extra handle
50	pounds cornmeal	1	dozen heavy socks	2	picks handsaw whipsaw
35	pounds rice	6	pairs wool mittens	1	shovel pack strap
24	pounds coffee	3	suits heavy underwear	6	files drawing knife brace and bits jack plane hammer chisels butcher knife
5	pounds tea	2	pairs Mackinaw trousers	3	
100	pounds sugar	2	pairs overalls	200ft	3/8 inch rope
25	pounds fish	2	hats	10	pounds pitch
15	pounds soup vegetables	4	heavy woolen overshirts	5	pounds oakum
50	pounds oatmeal	1	Mackinaw coat	2	caulking irons
50	pounds dried potatoes	1	heavy rubber-lined coat suspenders	15	pounds nails
50	pounds dried onions		Handkerchiefs		tent canvas
25	cans butter		snow glasses		whet stone
100	pounds beans	2	woolen blankets		compass
4	dozen tins condensed milk	2	oil blankets		goggles

15	pounds salt 1 pound pepper	4	towels buttons		quartz glass quicksilver
8	pounds baking powder		Thread & needles	2	frying pans
2	pounds baking soda	5	yards mosquito netting		coffee and tea pot
1/2	pound mustard	60	boxes of matches	40	pounds of candles eating plate, cup, knife
3/4	pound ginger	5	bars of soap.		fork, spoon pots & pans steel stove for 4 men gold pan gold scales
36	pounds yeast cakes				

Also additional items were noted, such as: medicines, reading matter, guns, ammunition and personal items.

It was, obviously, a monumental job to simply acquire the list of supplies, let alone get them transported to Lake Bennett to go by handmade rafts to the Klondike. I suspect the people who acquired and sold all the materials to prospective prospectors were the primary ones who made money as opposed to those who were going to the gold fields to mine. In reading about the gold rush I have discovered that there were several finds of gold from Southeast Alaska to the Klondike and it took place from about 1890 through 1910 with the biggest being the Klondike which was 1896 through 1900.

Roy and I fell in love with Skagway (as a tourist town). We enjoyed the train ride, which was different each time we went with its amazing switch backs and bridges and scenery. The first train ride was to Lake Bennett and concluded at the top with an old-fashioned beef pie lunch. The second trip was only halfway up to the lake and then back down. The third time we went up to the lake but didn't make a stop there and came back down. All of the tours were satisfying and we were glad to have made the trips. The first trip we made had a humorous ending. When we were nearing Skagway, we were told to have our passports ready because Canadian and U.S. customs would be checking passengers. I was panicked because I had not brought my purse with me from Skagway and it had all my ID in it. Roy shrugged when I asked him what I should do. So we got in the line and when I got to the agent I told him I hadn't brought ID with me when we left Skagway not thinking about crossing a border into another country. The agent looked at me and said "Where were you born?" I said, "Idaho." He said "Well, last I knew that was in the U.S. Have a nice day, ma'am. Thank you for coming to Canada." We've had a good laugh over that many times.

We did the whole tourist scene in Skagway, visiting all the places which were costumed and decorated as though it were 1898. We had a glorious time and managed to visit Skagway twice more in our life together. Roy had fond childhood memories of a summer spent in Skagway and he had so few fond memories of those days that he treasured re-living them with me. He told me stories and showed me all the places where he had had adventures. When we left Skagway in our boat heading south down Lynn Canal, it looked like good weather, but we hadn't checked the marine weather forecast until we were well on our way. There was a foul weather alert broadcast on the marine radio indicating it would be a good idea to seek shelter. All the fishing boats were scurrying into a port or anchorage. We started looking for a cove that would shelter us from the north wind. Looking at the chart for Lynn Canal, Roy decided to head for the small sheltered cove on Sullivan Island. We made it without any trouble and anchored up. The bottom was fine and caught our anchor perfectly. The sun was shining brightly and we were completely sheltered from the wind coming down Lynn Canal. It was so idyllic that we heated up some water and took complete sponge baths out in the cockpit of our boat, enjoying the sunshine and the long Alaska summer day. We were undoubtedly aided and abetted by the wind whistling down Lynn Canal keeping all the pleasure boat traffic from coming into our little hideaway anchorage. I will never forget that lovely afternoon.

The trip we made in the boat circumnavigating Chichagof Island was really enjoyable too. Actually all our boating was wonderful. There was only one Labor Day trip where we were not comfortable with the anchorage we chose. Roy worried about it sufficiently that he sat up all night on anchor watch. It ended up okay, but we never tried that anchorage again. Roy was always safety conscious. We only dragged anchor one time and that was in Pirate's Cove where apparently Roy felt safe because he didn't wake up when we started drifting. He was very embarrassed and unhappy when he discovered what was happening. We were soon under control and only had to cope with the comments made by other boats who had watched us drift and made comments on the marine radio about it. Otherwise, we never did that a second time ever. Our trip around Chichagof took us up the main route to Salisbury Sound and then we took off on the outside of Chichagof. Roy's remembrance was from boating in a very slow troller from years before, so we zoomed by the opening we needed to take up to Lisianski Strait. Roy quickly realized what had happened and got us back on track. We slipped through the passage between Yakobi Island and Chichagof and made stops at both Elfin Cove and Pelican, which I found very interesting. It was amazing to me in our explorations as to where people built structures to live in and made their environment comfortable and usable. Then we slipped across Icy Strait and found a place to anchor near the lodge in Glacier Bay. We bought two tours via commercial sight seeing vessels to see Glacier Bay. One of them was up the short arm of the Park and was a day trip; the other was up the longer bay and was an overnight trip. Neither one afforded us sunshine for the Park tour but it was absolutely stunning even with drizzly weather. I was entranced by the animals we saw and in those inlets which ended in a tidewater glacier there would be dozens of floating icebergs, on which seals were resting. It was a magic exploration and we enjoyed it to the fullest. We were given the opportunity to get out at one place and climbed up to the glacier face. Amazingly there was an abundance of wild flowers and vegetation. We spent 3 days in Glacier Bay and enjoyed every minute. The ice has melted significantly since that lovely summer so there are now other sights and animals to see and not the amazing amount of glaciers and the ice structures which we were so privileged to see. I have always been extremely grateful to have seen Glacier Bay before it retreated so far.

From Glacier Bay we went across Icy Strait to Hoonah and stopped there for a couple of hours before we headed back to Auk Bay. From

Auk Bay we scooted down to Peril Strait and then home again. Once again, we had a glorious time.

How fortunate I was to have Roy, who knew the waters and boats and marine navigation and enjoyed the adventures as much as I did. Roy told me many times to continue to appreciate the beautiful country that we lived in. It would be too easy to take it for granted and he didn't want me to ever do that. There was always something new to learn about our rain forest. My dad, who came up to go fishing with Roy every year until he was unable to make the trip, always was in awe of the green colors, every shade of green possible. I think being grateful for the beauty of nature was a part of my DNA. We always reminded each other that to get all that green color it required a lot of rain, so I learned never to be unhappy with rainy weather. We also twice experienced a spectacular show of marine mammals breaching, diving and feeding. Once was at Morris Reef at the entrance from Peril Strait to Chatham Strait when we saw dolphins, orcas and humpbacks performing an incredible show as far as we could see on the horizon. The second time was out at Biorka when the feeding frenzy extended oceanward as far as one could see. At Morris Reef it also included the orcas chasing a male sea lion. The orcas seemed to be working together as they circled the sea lion and killed it. It was definitely one of the most astonishing things I have seen in my years in Southeast Alaska. The female sea lions had gathered over in the kelp where the orcas didn't go. I've always thought about what huge schools of feed fish it took to provide that amazing show of marine mammals feeding. The aerial displays of mammals jumping out of the water was something never to be forgotten. Roy had turned our engines off and we were just drifting so we could watch without being noticed. We probably spent two or more hours watching each show. I've always hoped that harem of female sea lions attracted another magnificent male to lead their group. Roy, in his own fashion, thanked the male sea lion for providing food to the orcas. That was a huge bonanza for that pod of killer whales.

Roy always thanked the salmon or the lingcod or the clams for providing us with food. We live in a generous and kind, bountiful environment and have been continuously grateful for always having food to eat. We loved the Sitka deer too, but Roy didn't hunt. We enjoyed all the venison we received and understood Roy's reluctance to hunt those beautiful animals. Since I have been widowed, I seek someone to subsistence proxy hunt for me and remember to thank the animals for giving themselves to us for food.

We made one trip via cruise ship, which was a long-hoped-for dream come true. The year was 2004 and the ship was the Holland America's Oosterdam. I had retired from the school district and had collected my SBS in cash rather than an additional supplemental pension. I could have used it for the supplemental benefit but decided not to do so because I would have had to give up my ownership of that money and if something would have happened to me, whatever balance was left would go to the State. That bothered me because that was essentially money I had earned and invested with the State and I wanted to use it. I've always been glad I made that decision because Roy and I enjoyed the three week cruise so much and we allowed ourselves to be generous to ourselves, getting a stateroom on the next to top deck and taking advantage of all the amenities we were interested in. We wrote a travel log as we went along and sent it to our family from the ship via the internet. We took what was called the turnaround cruise. The ship had been taking Alaska cruises and was on its way to Fort Lauderdale to take Caribbean cruises during the winter. We went down the coast of Mexico, making four stops in Mexico, then Guatemala, Nicaragua and Costa Rica. Then we spent a full day going through the Panama Canal which was absolutely fascinating. Roy enjoyed it to the fullest, spending most of the day on the top deck looking at the workings of the canal. The canal uses a lake for the middle part of the trip across the Isthmus where we saw numerous tropical birds, along with crocodiles. There were professional naturalists who gave talks as we went along. The whole day was fascinating and we enjoyed every minute. I think Roy roasted himself like a chestnut in the hot tropical sun, staying outside so he wouldn't miss anything. It was way too hot for my puny body, so I stayed mostly in the stateroom where I could slip in and out of our private balcony to see everything. I have all the pictures and things we collected along the way and have always intended to make a scrapbook out of it for a memory. Of course, I haven't ever gotten it done and probably won't at this point, but everything is in a couple of boxes, so could easily be done at any time. When we left the Canal we went to Curacao which was our favorite port of the whole trip. It is about 19 miles north of the coast of Venezuela, with whom the Arubans have a treaty to handle the oil wells and oil, which Aruba sells to maintain its government. It sounds like a very unusual but successful way for both Aruba and Venezuela to export the oil and make money. I've never researched it, so I don't know much about the particulars of the arrangement.

Other than Aruba, which we found extremely interesting, the rest of the trip through the Caribbean was not hugely exciting. We visited the British Virgin Islands, which used U.S. money and seemed like visiting Los Angeles in a tropical setting, and the Bahamas. The only other Caribbean stop we made was to a small island owned by Holland America, which they had turned into a "tropical playground" for adults. There had been a hurricane through the area a short time prior to our visit, so the poor island was quite scoured.

The entire itinerary is printed below. It was definitely an once-in-a-lifetime vacation!

Day 1	Seattle		Departure 5 p.m.
Day 2	Vancouver B.C.	Arrival 8 a.m.	Departure 5 p.m.
Day 3	At sea		
Day 4	At sea		
Day 5	Los Angeles	Arrival 7 a.m.	Departure 5 p.m.
Day 6	Cruising Pacific Ocean		
Day 7	Cabo San Lucas	Arrival 12 noon	Departure 6 p.m.
Day 8	Mazatlan	Arrival 8 a.m.	Departure 6 p.m.
Day 9	Puerto Vallarta	Arrival 7 a.m.	Departure 8 p.m.
Day 10	Zihuatanejo, Mexico	Arrival 2 p.m.	Departure 10 p.m.

Day 11   Cruising Pacific Ocean

Day 12   Puerto Quetzal, Guatemala   Arrival 6 a.m.   Departure 6 p.m.

Day 13   San Juan del Sur, Nicaragua   Arrival 12 noon   Departure 6 p.m.

Day 14   Puntarenas City, Costa Rica   Arrival 7:30 a.m.   Departure 7 p.m.

Day 15   Cruising Golfo Dulce

Day 16   Cruising Panama Canal   Arrival 7 a.m.   Departure 5 p.m.

Day 17   Cruising Caribbean Sea

Day 18   Willemstad, Curacao   Arrival 8 a.m.   Departure 10 p.m.

Day 19   Cruising Caribbean

Day 20   Tortola, British Virgin Islands   Arrival 7 a.m.   Departure 5 p.m.

Day 21   Cruising Caribbean

Day 22   Half Moon Cay, Bahamas   Arrival 8 a.m.   Departure 4 p.m.

Day 23   Fort Lauderdale, Florida   Arrival 8 a.m.

Fax to ship at any time except when the ship is IN port. Oosterdam, Stateroom #7106

When we arrived in Fort Lauderdale we still had another week of vacation. Roy had always wanted to see the highway that went down to Key West, which was originally on an island but had been connected to the mainland by a highway that jumped from tiny island to tiny island, taking us to Key West. We had a distance to drive from Fort Lauderdale until we met up with this amazing section of highway, which was essentially a very long bridge jumping from one small island to the next. It reminded us greatly of the WWII causeway in Sitka linking small islands to one another from Japonski Island to Makhnati Island and is now The Fort Rousseau Causeway.

This is a series of eight interconnected islands located in Sitka, Alaska, and is part of the Sitka Naval Operating Base and U.S. Army Coastal Defenses National Historic Landmark. In addition to National Historic Landmark status, the fort's significance as the headquarters for the harbor defenses of Sitka during World War II also earned it designation as a State Historical Park in April 2008. There is no civilian access (road) to the Park but the successful listing of the islands of the Causeway as a National Historical Park insures its place in history. Jan and her family camped out on Kirushkin Island Artillery Control Center on their annual summer family camp out one year. The small rugged "road" that connects the islands in Sitka could be well-determined as man made, converging off what is now the airport runway. Many of the gun emplacements and buildings are still out there to be explored, although care must be taken when exploring, since it has not had any upgrading for safety done since it was built at the beginning of the war. Permission to hike the causeway in Sitka must be secured prior to going.

We thoroughly enjoyed the drive down to Key West. We had reservations made to stay for three days and we completely enjoyed it. We went on a couple of boat trips. One was a magical sunset cruise and the other was a supposed exploration of part of the Everglades. That one was very disappointing, since the boat went very fast and I was very warm. Fortunately the couple running the boat found me some goggles to protect my eyes or the burn I got would have been worse. I had also slathered myself with sun screen. In any event, we went to a little restaurant located on one of the mangrove islands being formed naturally by the tropical growth. It was actually a quite tasty lunch and a relief for me from the hot wind blowing us as we moved along. When we left Key West we went to Isla Mirada, where we had reservations for another three days. In Isla Mirada we went fishing and had a glorious time. The captain and his deckhand, a young man in his teens or early twenties, were pleasant and informative and thrilled to have as their clients of the day "an older couple." It was interesting to see how the charter fishermen there rigged the rods for us. We had very good luck and caught several fish, one of which was a dolphin fish, a flat-nosed fish that was quite prized for its flavor. We took that fish with us and went to a restaurant, where they prepared it for us for dinner and we feasted, ending up sated and very happy. The people at the restaurant assured us that someone would gladly take all the leftovers home for their family's dinner so we were glad of no waste.

After the week of exploring Key West, seeing a live butterfly exhibit, and the house that Hemingway lived in while he was in Key West as well as our incredible fishing trip in Isla Mirada, we drove back to Fort Lauderdale to fly home. What an amazing adventure we had!

We had one more incredible happening on the way back to the airport. Roy had lost his laptop - actually we thought he left it in the lobby at the car rental place. When we got to the car rental he went into the office to check on his laptop. I was totally skeptical about him ever getting it back. Good thing he was optimistic, because I would never have even checked! He disappeared into the area behind the customer service podiums out front. Out came the agent, who was helping him with a laptop in his hands. I saw Roy nodding his head and taking the computer. A few more words to the agent and Roy came out of the office with a big smile on his face! Wow! Did that blow me away! Big lesson: Always at least check when you've lost something valuable, even if you don't think there's any possibility. He always teased me about my pessimism, which he knew would aggravate me because of my belief that I'm an optimist but also a realist! So as a realist sometimes amazing things happen.

By 2008 Roy was having more and more problems with his balance and was afraid to take the boat out. We both missed our boating but it was better to heed Father Time's messages so we stayed close to shore. We went out very occasionally for a lunch break, but always stayed quite close to home, usually stopping and drifting in a cove close to Silver Point. Roy did not want to consider selling the boat. He told me "When a Tlingit man sells his boat it means he has decided his time is up." That broke my heart so I never mentioned it again. Roy thoroughly enjoyed going down to the boat and as he called it, "puttering." Mike Reif twice took us out fishing on his boat. That was wonderful. Mike knew we loved fishing out at Biorka, so that's where we went both times.

Both times there were humpbacks feeding out there and breaching to give us a wonderful show. We caught salmon – to me when I caught a "fish" I always meant a salmon. Roy always loved to tease me about all the "non-fish" we caught. But we always fished for salmon and very seldom for halibut. To be honest, I didn't like to jig. I preferred trolling, so I was probably the primary reason for that. The only time I ever got any inkling of sea sickness was when we jigged with the engines off, just drifting. Of course, that was the primary way to fish for halibut. They are bottom fish and you lower your bait to the bottom and let the drifting bring the bait up to a short distance off the bottom. We sometimes caught a halibut simply by trolling down close to the bottom. Daddy always liked to try for halibut just because he and Elaine really enjoyed eating it. One time Aaron was fishing with us and up at Kalinan Bay he caught a halibut by trolling close to the bottom. We were already anchored up in Kalinan Bay and so it was a pretty good sized one and gave Roy quite a tussle when he got it aboard. Aaron was afraid he was going to lose it, so he asked Roy to land it. Roy had to go around and around the gunwale of the boat and finally got it in. When we left Kalinan Bay to go home we left via the outside route, which brought us back to Sitka via Cape Edgecumbe. Roy had slowed down to trolling speed as we came up on the Cape and, amazingly, Aaron got another halibut on. That was a pretty exciting fishing trip, which we will never forget. Aaron took home two halibut and we also caught half a dozen cohos, so we were more than happy. We were doing our most favorite thing in the world: fishing from our boat.

By 2010 our lives were definitely slowing down. Roy had considerable trouble with his balance and he had developed a persistent cough, which troubled both of us a lot. We no longer could jump on the boat on a whim and go to one of the many fishing spots we enjoyed. Roy did not want to get rid of our boat; he loved going down to putter on it. Our doctor finally decided we needed to go south and see a pulmonologist at Virginia Mason, so we made those arrangements and jumped on an Alaska Airlines plane. Roy went through a long list of tests and found he had Stage 4 lung cancer. The tumor was tangled up in the primary blood vessels to the heart and had metastasized throughout his body. By the time we left Seattle they had told us that he had two to four months left. I asked him if he had someplace he'd like to go while he was still able to get around and he said "Maui", so I relayed that information to Jan. The oncologist we saw just before we left told me to make our Hawaii trip as soon as possible. Since Christmas was only a few days away, it would need to take place as early in January as possible. We were devastated and unfortunately I degenerated emotionally to being unable to do almost anything. Jan became our "go to" person, keeping the family informed. She had our Hawaii trip all planned and paid for by the time we landed in Sitka from Seattle. Roy didn't want to change anything about our living situation, wanting to try to be as close to normal as possible. That became almost impossible as family members wanted to come see Roy while he was still able to visit and started to make those arrangements immediately. Aaron and his wife, Carol, decided they wanted to remember Roy alive and happy so they opted to accompany us to Hawaii and Carol made all the hotel reservations at a new resort, on Maui close to where we had our honeymoon! It was a gorgeous apartment and Aaron and Carol took good care of us. Roy seemed to be extremely happy and enjoyed the trip immensely. On the day we were scheduled to leave they had a huge wind and rainstorm (shades of Sitka) which caused landslides and blocked the road to the airport. Aaron and Carol were okay because their flight left later than ours, but we were unable to get to the airport so we had to find a place to stay. Unfortunately, the apartment we had been staying in was not available unfortunately but Carol found us a place. It was definitely not plush, but for something in a pinch it was okay. Aaron and Carol got us moved. We took our rented wheelchair with us, which caused some consternation but which worked. I called Alaska Airlines and got our ticket changed. We managed fine and got out the following day without a problem. We had gone up the Maui volcano to see the sunrise just fine, which Roy was thrilled about. I still wonder if we really should have done that – it was 10,000 feet in elevation – but Roy being Roy never said a word, so we went up and he enjoyed the sunrise, which was definitely spectacular. We were treated to seeing some blooming cactus, which we were told didn't grow anywhere else other than this area on the volcano! It was a wonderful trip and Roy was very appreciative. Coming home was stressful for me, but it seems that when you have no alternatives, you put yourself together. I had arranged to borrow a hospital bed for Roy at home so it would be easier to take care of him. The home health nurses came to see him regularly and we tried, oh so hard, to keep up with the escalation of his pain he had. Jan essentially took the time off work and was there for Roy and all of us. For the first three weeks Roy took his pills and endeavored to keep a regular life, but he couldn't continue and started refusing pills, oxygen and everything else. Dr. Hunter came to see him once. Eventually he was unable to go to the bathroom by himself. All in all he was with us for seven weeks after his diagnosis. Almost all the family managed to come up to see him, for which I was grateful. Warren came later in the month. Both the Kimball's and the Vastola's donated places for the family to sleep. Pat Welch organized meals to be brought to us. The outpouring of assistance was almost overwhelming. I worried about Jan missing so much work, but she kept telling me she was okay and she really was needed and kept things organized and Roy comfortable. On February 12th, Roy lapsed into Cheyne-Stokes breathing and we knew he was going to leave us. Jan, Gayleen and I stayed beside him holding his hands and caressing him so he knew we were there. Anita was nearby. It was a peaceful departure, though I admit it felt like I had dropped off a mile high cliff. I did not realize it' but I fell into a deep depression, not wanting to eat or do much of anything other than continuing to sink into the depths of despair.

CHAPTER 12

My Fifth Life

Within two months, Jan had asked for and gotten my blessing on moving in with me and she had dragged me into my doctor's office to request help in combating my depression. I was not able to cry. Although I wanted to cry, I just felt unable. I hated the comments from well-meaning friends, for some reason feeling they were demeaning. I knew everyone wanted to give me love and consolation but it was very difficult to accept. Although I know now that my feelings of being totally set loose with no moorings or anchor to hold me were reasonably normal, at the time I was truly distraught and couldn't seem to put myself together. I couldn't sleep and I didn't eat appropriately, so I lost a lot of weight. I read a lot about bereavement and mourning and decided to go to the Lutheran Church. It seemed that getting some prayer help would be good for me and although I didn't know much about the Lutherans, I knew several people whom I admired who went to that church. I had gotten acquainted with the pastor when I was asked, by Harvey Brandt, to help the Finnish ambassador to the United States arrange a sight seeing itinerary for a visit here, which he was planning with connection to a conference on the Arctic and the many expected changes that were being predicted. That had happened prior to Roy's death, but it gave me an impetus to make this change, which I felt would be good for me. I felt completely welcomed to the church. There was no huge push to get me involved in various activities, so I was able to go and refresh myself with worship and music and quiet and it was immensely refreshing and healing. I have since joined in the fellowship and it has been a huge blessing. I feel accepted and cared for and allowed my space, which was particularly special to me. Thank you for the love I needed, Pastor Sandra.

As time has gone by I have finally fairly well adjusted to not having Roy in my life any more. I will always miss him terribly. He was truly the rock upon which I was anchored. He was an amazingly spiritual man who loved me deeply and who was always there for me. He always let me be me and I knew with no doubt ever that his love was always his gift to me, made with no strings attached and with strong and unbreakable love and care. We knew how much we meant to each other. We knew it was forever.

In 2013 Gayleen contacted me and said that Steve had moved out and no longer intended to live with her, so I made plans to fly to Dublin to visit and to bring her to Sitka to live with Jan and I. Patty Sexton, one of the Nanney cousins to my children, helped us fill in the paperwork for her to receive financial assistance and medical care. It took us about to the end of the year to get accepted so she could get the medical care she needed. She's been with us for over two years now and she's done wonderfully. She sees a psychiatrist regularly, along with her primary care physician, and has weathered having her gall bladder removed, as well as surgery removing a benign tumor from near her ear, as well as a complete revamping of her medicine. She is completely off lithium now and has had adjustments made on almost all of her medications. She is very happy with all the changes, is happy with the counseling she is getting and essentially has her moods stabilized and is maintaining very well. We all get along reasonably well and seem able to talk through any difficulties we have.

Gayleen has completed divorce proceedings, feeling that in order to make a new life for herself she needed to close that chapter. On September 10th 2015, the hearing for final dissolution was held with Steve phoning in for the hearing from Budapest, where he now lives. The marriage was finished with the judge declaring the dissolution permanent. Jan went with Gayleen to the court hearing. She seems to be adjusting although she had some tearful times after coming home from the courthouse. She is determined to find joy in her individual life now. She is a beautiful, kind and adventurous woman with a future still to come.

This has brought us to the end of The Hundred Year Stretch which I hope has shown the many ups and downs that life brought us and the joy that I believe should continue to ensue when part of our lives has changed dramatically as we find the pathway through our hopes and dreams which continue. Change happens and can bring happiness and new ideas and joys. All of us can allow those new ideas and joys to sustain us if we expect them. Expectation can be a great teacher.

I love my current life, even with knowing that Roy is gone but will be my love forever.

Doris Chapin Bailey

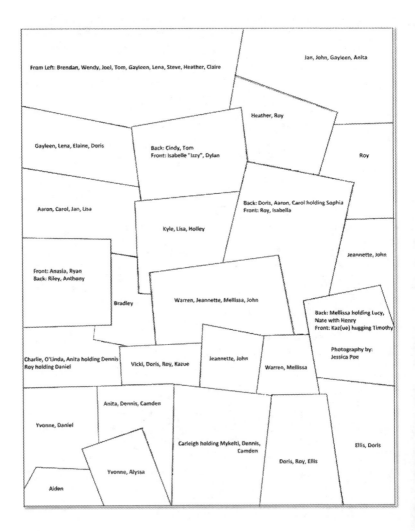

From Left: Brendan, Wendy, Joel, Tom, Gayleen, Lena, Steve, Heather, Claire

Jan, John, Gayleen, Anita

Heather, Roy

Gayleen, Lena, Elaine, Doris

Back: Cindy, Tom
Front: Isabelle "Izzy", Dylan

Roy

Aaron, Carol, Jan, Lisa

Back: Doris, Aaron, Carol holding Sophia
Front: Roy, Isabella

Kyle, Lisa, Holley

Jeannette, John

Front: Anasia, Ryan
Back: Riley, Anthony

Bradley

Warren, Jeannette, Mellissa, John

Back: Mellissa holding Lucy,
Nate with Henry
Front: Kaz{ue} hugging Timothy

Photography by:
Jessica Poe

Charlie, O'Linda, Anita holding Dennis
Roy holding Daniel

Vicki, Doris, Roy, Kazue

Jeannette, John

Warren, Mellissa

Anita, Dennis, Camden

Yvonne, Daniel

Carleigh holding Mykelti, Dennis,
Camden

Ellis, Doris

Yvonne, Alyssa

Doris, Roy, Ellis

Aiden

Printed in the United States
By Bookmasters